An Oregon Legal Guides book

Oregon's Legal Guide for College Students

An Oregon Legal Guides book

Oregon's Legal Guide for College Students

Janay Haas, JD

Check www.oregonlegalguides.com for periodic updates.

ISBN: 978-0-9851922-3-5 (Paperback)

ISBN: 978-0-9851922-2-8 (Digital)

CONTENTS

WHY THIS GUIDE?

In Oregon, about one college student in 10 has at least one legal problem while in school. Dealing with those problems can be discouraging and demoralizing—and can cost a lot of money. For some students, a legal problem can mean dropping out of school, in some cases for a long time. Knowing what the rules are as you start your college career can make a big difference in your ability to make good decisions and prevent legal difficulties. **This guide can help you prevent legal problems, so read it sooner rather than later. This guide can also help you quickly identify *when* you have a legal problem that will require the help of a lawyer.**

Once you turn 18, you're an adult in the eyes of the law. And as a college student, you'll be making personal decisions and commitments that will affect your legal rights and duties. Living in a dorm? You'll have to sign a legally binding contract to live there and do what the contract says. Moving into a rental, on your own or with roommates? Landlord-tenant law will apply to you. Signing up for utilities, cell phone, and Internet service? Buying a car or taking out student loans? Laws about contracts and consumer rights will apply to those transactions.

Together, these transactions will build your "credit history," a record of financial reliability that will make it easier—or harder—for you to buy a home or rent an apartment, get affordable car insurance, or get a job. As you enter the job market and begin to build your career, you will need to learn about your rights as an employee and about the rights that employers have in the workplace.

Then there's your sex life: What's consensual sex? What's not? What do you do about the "friend" who gave you a sexually transmitted infection (STI)? Or the violent partner? Or the creep who follows you all the time or puts embarrassing photos of you on the Internet? What happens if you or your partner becomes pregnant? If you're in a relationship or have kids, the law will affect you.

What if you're stopped by the police? About a third of the legal problems that campus lawyers see are the result of criminal charges against students: drunk driving; minor in possession of alcohol or drugs; public intoxication; assault and hazing; invasion of privacy; and lots more conduct that "seemed like a good idea at the time." Nobody wants to be remembered as that fool who lost a full scholarship because he drunkenly knocked over a campus port-a-potty after the Big Game. And humiliation is the easy part; taking care of the problem in court will be expensive. A criminal record will dog you for a long time, too, complicating your life in a whole range of ways.

This handbook may be able to point you to some guidance if you already have a legal problem. It can't solve your legal problem for you, though. So look at the "Appendix 1: Getting Help" at the end of this guide that may help you further.

Remember two things: (1) the law changes frequently; and (2) no general guide like this one can tailor information to your specific circumstances. If you identify something as a legal problem, or if something just feels unfair to you, always seek the advice of an attorney. Don't wait; unlike some other problems, legal problems almost never go away. They just get worse. And exercising your rights and finding a solution can require quick action on your part.

Visit www.oregonlegalguides.com for updates on the general topics in this guide.

A.

WHERE YOU LIVE AND THE LAW

A-1. Dorm Life and the Law

Living in a dorm has plusses and minuses. If you live in a dorm, you signed an agreement with the school to follow certain rules. If you don't follow the rules, you can be brought before the student housing or disciplinary board, and, worst case, be removed from the dorm and the campus meal plan you paid for—without getting your money back.

Not all on-campus housing contracts are identical, so read what you signed if you didn't read it before you signed. Typical contracts prohibit using drugs of any kind. Note that using marijuana may be legal under state law, but it's not legal under federal law, the law that colleges and universities must follow. Using alcohol is also prohibited if you're under age 21. Other prohibited items typically include guns, long-term guests who aren't paying to stay in your dorm room, pets, hot plates and open flames, harassment, and sexual assault and other violence.

The school has a duty to keep campus housing safe for all. Your contract undoubtedly gives staff permission to enter your room to make sure there are no fire or safety hazards or rule violations. If staff find contraband in your room, they are NOT authorized to let police come into your room. Their authority is limited to reporting rule violations to the student housing or disciplinary office. If police show up, you do not have to let them into your room if they do not show you a warrant. If you have a roommate, make sure that person doesn't invite the police in, either.

A-2. Fraternity and Sorority Housing

Like living in a campus dorm, living in fraternity and sorority housing requires you to sign a contract. This kind of housing, which usually includes a meal plan, typically does not have to abide by Oregon's Landlord Tenant Law.

Similar to a dorm contract, the fraternity or sorority housing contract will contain a list of rules that you must follow. The club can force you to move out if you don't comply with the rules in the contract. On some campuses, the process of getting you out of the fraternity or sorority house may involve the student disciplinary board; on other campuses, the school itself may not be involved.

The contract may require you to pay up front for your lodging for the entire term or the entire school year. The contract may not give you the right to get a refund of any of that money if you move out, regardless of the reason.

If the contract is labeled a lease, however, and if the housing is off-campus, you may have tenant rights after all. Determining your rights can be difficult, so get legal advice before giving up big money when you leave.

A-3. Rental Housing and the Law

Most students are first-time renters. Most are young. Most don't know the laws they have to follow to be good tenants. In short, most landlords would rather rent to somebody else.

Common complaints that landlords have about younger renters, students among them, include:

1. Other tenants and neighbors complain about parties, loud music, and general rowdiness;
2. The police get called;
3. Young tenants ignore the "no pets" policy;
4. Students with loans spend their money on things besides necessities, and end up owing rent before the end of the school year (see budgeting tips in Section B-7); and

5.   Young tenants tend not to have mops or vacuum cleaners or cleaning supplies, so they leave their unit filthy when they move out.

As you can see, persuading certain landlords to rent to you may not be easy. Don't get discouraged, though. Be courteous, offer good references, and you'll get a chance to prove you can be a successful tenant. A positive tenant experience will mean a good reference from this landlord the next time you want to rent.

Does the law cover you? The Oregon Residential Landlord and Tenant Act (ORLTA) applies to rental houses and apartments, and rooms and "house shares" in other people's homes. These are the most common housing situations, so the law described below applies to them.

Other parts of ORLTA apply to living in a hotel room, in a mobile home on rented private land, houseboat space rentals, and mobile home parks where the tenant owns the mobile home. Those less-common situations are *not* discussed here. In addition, recreational vehicles in an RV or mobile home park and "drug-free" housing for people in recovery follow different rules, as do student "co-ops" and dorm or fraternity-sorority living.

Landlord-tenant law is complex. Not knowing your duties and rights can result in speedy eviction, negative credit and tenant history reports, and other unpleasant and dangerous things—like living in your car.

Housing covered by ORLTA is subject to anti-discrimination laws that can protect current tenants and applicants for housing, too. See Section A-15 for important information about your rights against discrimination.

The topics below are a general outline; specific situations may rely on several ORLTA provisions. The City of Portland also has ordinances that affect landlord and tenant rights in that city; those aren't outlined here.

COVID-19 tip: So many people lost their incomes during the pandemic that the state of Oregon suspended tenants' duty to pay rent from April 1 until September 30, 2020. In September 2020, the state continued the April-September rent moratorium until January 1, 2021. As of October 2020, landlords cannot charge late fees for the April-September period or attempt to evict for nonpayment. Landlords are liable for damages for violating this law. Starting January 2021, tenants must pay full rent again plus enough money to make up for earlier unpaid rent for April-September by March 31, 2021. Tenants who do not tell the landlord they plan to use the grace period to catch up may be liable for a half-month's rent penalty. However, unless the legislature changes the law about the October-December extension, any unpaid rent for those months will be due January 1, 2021. It is likely that landlords will make mistakes about how much is due and when. See a lawyer to learn and enforce your rights.

A-4. Your Duties as a Tenant

Tenants and their landlords have both duties and rights. As a tenant, your duties include:

1. Paying the full rent due, on time;
2. Using the unit only as a home (not as a business, legal or illegal);
3. Avoiding damage to the unit and keeping it reasonably clean;
4. Promptly reporting the need for repairs to the landlord (see Section A-8, "Landlord's Duty to Provide Safe and Decent Housing," for more details);
5. Testing and replacing batteries on smoke alarms and carbon monoxide alarms;
6. Following reasonable rules that the landlord imposes;
7. Respecting the rights of other tenants and neighbors to a quiet and peaceful life;
8. Letting the landlord come in after you have asked for repairs or after the landlord has given reasonable notice (see Section A-13, "Your Right to Privacy"); and

9. At the end of your tenancy, giving back the keys and returning the unit to your landlord in the same condition you found it, except for normal wear and tear.

Take photos of your rental unit when you move in, and save the photos where you can find them when you move out. See Section A-6, "Security Deposits," for more information.

A-5. Roommates

Should you have a roommate or two to cut your living expenses? Sharing housing can be an effective way to manage your budget—but there are risks to consider before you make this commitment.

Signing your rental agreement. The name of every housemate should be on your lease. Generally, each named tenant on a lease is wholly responsible for all damage to an apartment regardless of who caused it. If your roommate is not named on the lease, you and any other roommates who are named are legally responsible for the full amount of the rent and for any damage to the rental. If you let someone move in without the landlord's advance permission, you likely will be risking eviction—of everyone in the unit. If a roommate moves out, you should inform your landlord and have the name removed from the lease.

Some landlords will permit each tenant to pay a portion of a security deposit. Make sure to ask the landlord for receipts for any security deposits that you pay. Some landlords will charge each roommate for only that person's share of the rent.

Bills. Sometimes one roommate will set up all the utility accounts for an apartment in one name. That's a bad idea: that roommate will bear all the financial and legal responsibility for those bills. Instead, each roommate should set up and pay for one or two of the utilities, with the goal of each roommate's taking responsibility for the same dollar amount each month. Set a schedule each month to calculate what's owed, and reimburse the roommates who spent more.

Buying things. You and your roommates should avoid making purchases together. For example, rather than splitting the cost of a sofa, one roommate should pay for the sofa while another pays for other household items. This way, when a roommate moves out, you can avoid a dispute over who gets to take furniture or other items. Be sure to keep a record of who owns that sofa or other items to avoid later disputes.

Buying your own food. It is unlikely that you and your roommates will make all meals together. It's easiest for each roommate to pay separately for food. Designate space in the fridge and cupboard for each roommate, and label items if necessary. Roommates should agree not to eat each other's food.

Your privacy. Before you move in or soon after, you and your roommates should discuss how you will live together. You should establish expectations for who will clean the apartment, how often, and when, and who will handle various chores such as taking out the trash and recycling. If a roommate has a pet, you should define who will feed and otherwise take care of the pet, and who will pay for any damage that the pet may cause to the apartment. You may also want to decide when guests may visit or stay in the apartment, and how you and your room-mates will communicate and agree on visits by guests. Finally, you may want to define what will happen if a roommate breaks one of these rules. Writing down these "House Rules" or drafting a roommate agreement with these terms can help ensure that all roommates understand what the expectations are for living together.

Illegal drugs and alcohol. If you have roommates under age 21 who have liquor, or roommates of any age who have any illegal drugs (including prescription drugs not prescribed to them), insist that they keep those items locked up in their own rooms. If police who have the right to enter your home (because they have a warrant, or because someone invites them in) may arrest you as well as the offending roommates for what could be drug felonies if there's contraband anywhere in your home that you have access to. Be sure your housemates and guests understand what can happen to all of you if one of them invites the police into your home. See Section G-2, "Alcohol and Drugs," for more information.

Considering these issues up front can help avoid conflicts, and make living with roommates much easier while you are in school.

A-6. Security Deposits

Landlords usually charge incoming tenants a "security deposit." It's money that belongs to the tenant but the landlord keeps it until the end of the tenancy. The outgoing tenant then gets back the money—minus the cost, if any, of unpaid rent or cleaning and repairs that the landlord must do to make the unit fit to rent again. Most landlords want the entire security deposit up front; a few landlords may allow you to pay it in addition to your rent for two or three months once you move in.

Some landlords won't return your security deposit even if you leave the unit in pristine condition; that's illegal, of course. Occasionally a landlord will charge a non-refundable "cleaning fee" rather than a security deposit—meaning you won't get your money back no matter what; that's illegal, too.

How can you protect your security deposit? The answer to this question starts as soon as you enter into the rental agreement. Your landlord should give you a receipt for your deposit, and the receipt should say how the deposit may be used (repairs only; repairs and unpaid rent; etc.). If the receipt does not specify a use, it can be used for unpaid rent and repairs. If your rental agreement allows the landlord to email the receipt or enter it into an online tenant portal, make sure you get it. Keep your proof of payment until you have moved out and gotten your deposit back.

Next, walk through the new place with a witness who isn't going to live there, inspect the unit, make notes about anything that is broken, scratched, dirty, moldy, stained, or missing—and take pictures (or even videos). Your inspection photos should include ceilings, stove tops, the outside *and* inside of sinks, showers, bath-tubs, toilets, refrigerators and ovens, dishwashers, washers and dryers, walls, closets, doors, windows, and floors (torn linoleum or carpets, etc.). Save these pictures. Also check faucets for leaks and hot water, heaters, air filters, smoke alarms and carbon monoxide alarms (and new batteries), missing or weak railings, and other things that might be the source of problems even if you can't photograph the problem.

If you do find problems, write to your landlord right away to ask for repairs. (See Section A-10, "Landlord's Duty to Provide Safe and Decent Housing," for what the landlord legally has to repair). Keep a copy of your letter, e-mail, or other communication. (If your rental agreement says how to give notices to your landlord, use that method.)

To ensure that you have the best chance of getting your entire security deposit back at the end of your tenancy, try to keep the unit in the condition it was in when you moved in. For example, if you plan to hang posters and pictures, look for temporary adhesive rather than making nail holes in walls—you'll be glad later on.

When the time gets close for you to move out, you must give the landlord at least 30 days' written notice of your intent to move. If you want to move out before the end of a term lease and if the landlord doesn't have an acceptable replacement tenant immediately, you can be charged a penalty of 150 per cent of a month's rent. See Section A-7, "Types of Rental Agreements," for more information.

Check whether your rental agreement requires you to steam-clean carpets when you move out. (Steam-cleaning is NOT the same as shampooing.) If you signed an agreement to do that, the landlord can hold back part of the security deposit if you don't. If you don't have cleaning supplies, borrow or rent them so you can clean thoroughly before move-out. You can also hire a professional carpet cleaner, who will give you a receipt. Note that some written rental agreements give the landlord the right to steam-clean whether you do or not and to charge you for it. Get a couple of photos of yourself as you're cleaning and, if you bought cleaning supplies or rented cleaning equipment, keep the receipts. If you have to go to court to get your money back, having this documentation will bolster your claim.

Invite the landlord to inspect the place when you move out. Conscientious land-lords often will agree to your invitation. Have a witness on hand for the inspec-tion. Ask if there's anything else you need to do in order to get your full security deposit back. Take the same thorough photographs that you took when you moved in so there will be no question about the condition of the place. Be sure to turn in your keys, and give the landlord (dated and in writing) your new address (again, keep a copy of your written communication) so that the landlord can refund all or part of your security deposit.

Your landlord has 31 days after you move out in which to return all of your security deposit, or to keep part or all of your deposit with a detailed explanation of why the money was needed to clean or repair something. The amount that the landlord keeps should be reasonable for the work done or for the work that the landlord estimates it will cost to do. If the receipt from the landlord said the deposit could be used for unpaid rent, that amount should appear on the itemized list, too. You may get a claim from the landlord for damage you didn't do or the cleaning of things that weren't dirty. In that case, politely inform the landlord in writing of the inspection you made and the photos you have, demanding the return of your money. Keep the landlord's letter and the envelope it came in.

If you haven't received anything from the landlord a month or so after you have moved out, it's time to write the landlord to repeat your new address, politely demand your money, and, if the landlord said so at inspection, repeat that the landlord said there was nothing else you needed to do in order to get your money back. Mention that you have a witness to the condition of the place at move-out and that you took photographs. Give the landlord a reasonable deadline to return your money (10 to 14 days is long enough). Keep a copy of the letter you send.

If you still don't hear anything or get your money back, you are prepared to make a case in small claims court. With your witness, photographs, and proof of your good-faith efforts to get the landlord to cooperate, you should be eligible to get your money back, along with a monetary penalty against the landlord who has acted in bad faith. Get legal advice to help you organize your case. You have a year and 31 days after you move out in which to file your case. See Section H-2, "Small Claims Court," for more information about using the court to get back your deposit and penalties, and Appendix 1, "Getting Help," for legal help. Read Oregon Legal Guides' *Using Small Claims Court in Oregon* for tips on preparing yourself and other witnesses for the courtroom.

The process will be more complicated if you have roommates and you move out before they do. If you haven't arranged with the landlord to have individual deposits, you may not be entitled to a refund until everyone in the unit moves out. In that case, you'll want to educate your co-renters about what they need to do to get the full deposit back when they move—or get them to reimburse you for your share when you go. Moving out first means that your evidence of how good the place looked when you left is even more important. You may find out later that, at the end-of-the-year party, people completely trashed the place. Your photos, receipts, and witnesses can keep you from getting stuck with a huge bill for repairs.

A-7. Types of Rental Agreements

Oregon offers two basic types of rental agreements: month-to-month, in which the tenancy goes on until the landlord or the tenant ends it (after proper notice); and fixed-term leases, which can end on a certain date without notice. Then the landlord and the tenant can decide whether to enter into a new agreement, or even to change the contract to month-to-month. See Section A-16, "When You Want to Move Out", for particulars.

In some places where rental units empty out when students leave for the summer, landlords may push for year-long leases so that the units produce income all summer long, even if the students aren't there.

A-8. Rent Hikes

In 2019, Oregon instituted "rent control." The new law doesn't do much for tenants. Here's what it does do:

In either a month-to-month rental or a fixed-term tenancy, your landlord can't raise the rent during the first year of your tenancy. After the first year, a rent hike can take effect on a stated date that is at least 90 days after written notice to the tenant. The rent can be raised only one time per 12-month period, with some exceptions.

There's a limit to how much the landlord can increase the rent—7 per cent plus the "consumer price index" above the previous rent. This isn't much of a limit, as you might guess. The rent-control law doesn't even apply to rentals in buildings under 15 years old.

Some landlords will use a rent hike or try to evict a tenant to retaliate against a tenant for exercising legal rights. If you believe that's what's happening in your case, see a lawyer as soon as possible.

Special note for Portland tenants: Since 2017, the City of Portland has required landlords to cover tenant relocation expenses ($2900 to $4500, depending on rental unit size) if they increase the rent more than 10 percent in a 12-month period. **COVID-19** made a temporary change. From mid-September 2020 through March 2021, landlords who raise the rent in any amount must offer relocation funds to a tenant who moves out regardless of the amount of the rent increase.

A-9. Landlord Rules

Oregon landlords can impose rules in addition to the terms of the rental agreement. The rules must be clear, reasonable, and not arbitrary or retaliatory. The rules must promote the safety, welfare, or convenience of the tenants; be designed to prevent abuse of the landlord's property; or distribute facilities or services fairly (although not necessarily equally) to tenants. The rules must tell tenants what to do to comply with them.

Rules must always be in writing. Tenants are entitled to know what the rules are when they enter into the rental agreement—or as soon as rules are adopted after the tenants have moved in. If a rule significantly changes the terms of the rental agreement, it can't apply to existing tenants unless they agree to it in writing.

One common rule is that tenants must have renter's insurance, giving the landlord the right to be notified by the insurance company if the coverage lapses. This rule should apply only to tenants whose income is above 50 per cent of local median income adjusted for family size. Student loans are not income. See the Oregon Housing Stability Council website for current limits:
https://www.oregon.gov/ohcs/pages/research-income-rent-limits.aspx

Some tenants with certain kinds of government rent subsidies are exempt from renter insurance rules, too. Landlords who violate this law or who file baseless claims are subject to a lawsuit for damages.

Some landlords use rules to limit the number of people allowed to live in the unit. In a few cases, limiting the number of people can have the effect of discriminating against families with children. Rules must allow at least two persons per bedroom, and more than that if the rooms are large. A room that is at least 70 square feet and has a fire exit can count as a bedroom even if the landlord calls it something else. If you think that a landlord may be using rules improperly to limit the number of people in the unit, get legal advice about your rights. See Section A-15, "Housing Discrimination," for more information.

A-10. Landlord's Duty to Provide Safe and Decent Housing

Oregon landlords must provide you with housing that's fit to live in—that is, "habitable"—no matter how low the rent is. To be habitable, your unit must:

1. Be free of rodents and bugs when you move in;
2. Have adequate, safe, and proper heating, plumbing, and electrical wiring for the full term of your tenancy (in other words, your landlord has the duty to maintain and repair these services);
3. Have a working smoke alarm always, and a working carbon monoxide alarm if there's gas, wood, kerosene, coal, or oil heat; a gas water heater or stove; or a garage that opens into the unit;
4. Have enough hot and cold running water for reasonable uses, with the water being safe to drink;
5. Be waterproof and weatherproof (no leaking ceilings, no daylight showing around outside doors or wind blowing through closed windows);
6. Have working locks for all outside doors and working latches for all windows;
7. Have trashcans and a trash collection service;
8. Be clean and safe for normal uses at the start of the tenancy; and
9. Have floors, walls, ceilings, stairways, and railings in good repair.

If the rental comes with a stove, refrigerator, dishwasher, fans, or air conditioning, the landlord must maintain those appliances in good repair. If you live in a building with other rental units, the landlord is responsible for keeping the "common areas" (halls, elevators, stairs, play areas, laundry areas, pools and exercise rooms, and other spaces open to all tenants) clean and safe for their normal and foreseeable uses, too.

State law does not require landlords to provide recycling services for tenants. In some cities (including Portland), some apartment complexes must provide recycling services. Check with your city government for the recycling requirements for your apartment complex.

A-11. When Repairs Are Needed

If your rental has a habitability problem, it is important to notify the landlord as soon as possible—by telephone and letter (or other ways agreed to in your rental agreement) to ask for repairs. Communicating in writing and keeping a copy of your letter, e-mail, or other communication is the best way to protect yourself if the landlord refuses to follow the law. In your letter, you can give the landlord a range of times that would be convenient for you for the repairs to be made; otherwise, the landlord or workers can enter at any reasonable time of day for the next seven days after the landlord gets your letter. (For more information about the landlord's right to enter, see Section A-13, "Your Right to Privacy.") If the problem is serious—burst water pipes, sewage backup, lack of heat in winter, no water, etc.—you should get legal advice immediately about how to proceed.

Can you withhold rent if your home isn't habitable? The answer is "Yes, but—." The law is complicated and you should not withhold rent unless you talk to a lawyer first. You also should know that withholding rent does not mean you can spend your rent money on something else. You may need to show a court that you had the rent money and still have the money to pay—so a judge doesn't conclude you just couldn't pay your rent when it was due.

For any habitability problem, take pictures, keep notes about what happened and when it happened, make notes about the landlord's response, and save damaged property in case you need to produce it in court to prove the damages you suffered. Speaking of court, remember that any e-mail or letter you send, or phone message you leave, may wind up being evidence in a legal case involving your landlord. Anything you say or write should be clear, polite, and business-like.

A-12. Paying for Utilities

Although your landlord has a legal duty to provide adequate, safe, and proper heating and plumbing and to ensure that your housing is waterproof and weather-proof (see Section A-10, "Landlord's Duty to Provide Safe and Decent Housing"), your landlord normally does not have a duty to pay your utility bills. In fact, most lease agreements provide that you will pay for your utility bills. If those bills are extraordinarily high through no fault of the landlord, you can't force your land-lord to insulate your unit or improve the efficiency of your furnace.

Some utilities offer bill-payment assistance programs, particularly in the win-ter months. If you're struggling to pay your heating bills, check with your local utility about those programs. See also Section B-3, "Heat, Lights, Water, Phone, Internet," for what to do if your utilities are shut off.

You may find that you have been paying not only for your own utilities, but also for utilities of other tenants in the same building. Your landlord cannot charge you for utility service to anyone else without advance written notice.

Your landlord has a legal duty to protect your unit from wind and rain. If your home isn't protected from drafts and water seepage, or if you believe you are paying someone else's utility bills, you will want to contact a lawyer for help.

If you live in a place where there is only one utility bill for all the units, the landlord can bill each unit to reimburse it for the cost. If the landlord provides cable/satellite TV, or Internet service, it can add a service charge to the amount of each unit's bill.

A-13. Your Right to Privacy

When you are a renter, the general rule is that your landlord does not have the right to enter your home—whether you have paid rent or not, whether the landlord is tak-ing you to court or not. There are some exceptions to this rule. One exception is that the landlord can enter to make reasonable inspections or repairs or show the place to potential buyers or renters, but only after the landlord has given you at least 24 hours' advance notice. The landlord can enter without advance notice in an emer-gency—flooding caused by broken pipes, a fire, a burglar on the premises, etc., but only if the landlord then gives you notice of that entry as soon as practicable afterwards. The most common exception to the general rule is if you have asked the landlord to make repairs. See Section A-11, "When Repairs Are Needed," for details.

If the landlord shows up uninvited or the landlord's conduct is unreasonable, you can deny entry. But remember, *you* have to act reasonably. You can't refuse to let the landlord in just to interfere with the landlord's exercising his or her rights or duties.

A-14. "My landlord took my stuff and locked me out!"

It's rare for landlords these days to take tenant belongings to force them out or to claim the items in lieu of unpaid rent, but it still happens. There is a fast process in your county circuit court where you can demand your belongings back, but often, talking to a lawyer is the best way to solve your problem. (It helps if you have a list and photos of your belongings, too, just as it's helpful to have this kind of information if you need to make a claim on renter's insurance.)

As for lockouts, those aren't as common as they used to be, either, probably because there are legal penalties landlords must pay if they don't use the court eviction process. If you find the landlord has locked you out of your unit, however, try first to convince the landlord it's not worth the penalty, and then get help from a lawyer if you still need it. If you need to get back in the same day, you do have the right to have a locksmith come and let you back in (save the receipt for court!), or, as a last resort, break in, so long as you do so with a minimum of damage to the unit. Get legal advice regardless, as soon as you can.

A-15. Housing Discrimination

Discrimination in housing occurs when a landlord, a lender, or an agent or advertiser treats someone or a group differently from the way it treats others in similar circumstances. This conduct is illegal if it is done based on the "protected status" of the person or others with whom that person associates.

What is protected status? Historically, groups of people have been treated unfairly when seeking housing. In response, federal, state, and even local laws have required that all persons get the same treatment and the same level of service, and the same ability to use and enjoy their home. To ensure that happens, the laws allow for sanctions against housing providers who discriminate against people on the basis of their race, sex, sexual orientation, disability, family status, national origin, color, religion, or source of income (such as welfare or disability benefits). In Oregon, another group with protected status is victims of domestic violence, sexual assault, or stalking. See Section F, "Crimes of Domestic Violence and Stalking," for your rights as a tenant in that situation. Oregon law also protects the rights of active-duty members of the military to break leases on short notice without penalty if they have orders to deploy.

Family status: Family status includes being married (including same-sex marriage), living together, having children, being pregnant, or adopting. Some landlords discriminate against children by unreasonably limiting the number of people who can live in a unit. See Section A-9, "Landlord Rules," for more information.

Disability status: Disability status includes both physical and mental disabilities. It also includes the landlord's perception that you have a disability, whether you do or not. If you have a guide dog, or other service animal or companion animal because of a medically documented disability, a landlord cannot refuse to rent to you on that basis or charge you a special deposit for that service animal or companion animal. The animal must behave itself, however. In the same vein, if you need to modify doorways or a bathtub or shower or countertops for a wheelchair in order to use your rental, a landlord must permit you to do that—at your own expense if it's a private landlord, but at government expense in low-income units. In privately owned rental housing, you also have the duty to return the unit to its previous condition if the modifications you made hurt the rental value. For example, if you removed a bathtub to create a roll-in shower, the modification probably wouldn't be a problem for future renters. If you lowered the cabinets, sink, and stove in the kitchen for use by someone using a wheelchair, the modifications likely would be a problem for future renters and you would have to restore those items to their standard heights when you move out.

Source of income: Oregon makes it illegal for landlords to discriminate against a prospective tenant or a tenant based on the source of that person's income (such as welfare or disability benefits).

Student status: Some landlords refuse to rent to students simply because they are students. This kind of discrimination has not yet been declared illegal in Oregon. For students who rely on loans to pay their rent, it *may* constitute discrimination based on source of income if the landlord is aware of your income source.

If you think a housing provider has discriminated against you, keep records of everything that has happened. See a lawyer. Talk to the Oregon Fair Housing Council about your options. See Appendix I, "Getting Help."

A-16. When You Want to Move Out

If your rental agreement is month-to-month, you'll need to give written notice to the landlord that you plan to leave at least 30 days in advance. If you have room-mates and you are not all moving out at the same time, you will need to make clear in your notice that it applies only to you.

After giving proper notice, you are liable for rent only until the move-out date. If you paid "last month's rent" when you moved in, the landlord is to apply that money to your remaining time in the rental.

For those with a term lease who want to move out, the procedure is the same—unless you want to move out early. In that case, the landlord can force you to pay a penalty of 45 days' rent.

A-17. When Your Landlord Wants You to Move Out

A landlord can end your tenancy for any legal reason. What is legal depends on the circumstances. For instance, it is never legal to terminate a tenancy:

- — In retaliation for complaints about habitability problems;
- — Because you are pregnant or have children;
- — Because of discrimination based on your race, religion, color, ethnic background, sex, family status, or sexual orientation;
- — Because of the source of your income;
- — Because you are a victim of domestic violence, sexual assault, or stalking; or
- — Because you go on active military duty.

If you have a month-to-month tenancy and have lived in your rental for up to one year, the landlord can terminate the rental agreement without stating the reason (so long as it's a legal reason) on 30 days' written notice. If the notice is mailed but is not posted at your unit, the notice from the landlord should tell you that you have three extra days in which to move based on the additional time for mailing. Your landlord may choose to post a notice in a designated location only if you originally agreed to this arrangement in a written rental agreement.

The landlord also can ask you to move for "good cause"—that is, claiming that you have violated the rental agreement or written rules in some way. In most instances, you have the right to fix ("cure") the problem that the landlord cited so you can stay in the unit. If you have a term lease or have lived in your rental for more than a year, the landlord can end the lease only for good cause; again, in most cases you have the right to cure the problem and stay in your home. If you violate a term of the lease or landlord rules a second time, you can be fined up to $50 for most violations, up to $250 for smoking in a non-smoking place.

Late or unpaid rent is by far the most common reason that landlords end tenancies. In many cases, tenants simply spent their rent money on something else—often something less important than having a place to live. If you worry about having enough money to pay your rent, you can avoid or at least reduce the likelihood of eviction by carefully budgeting. See Section B-7 for some quick tips on handling money wisely. Free help with budgeting also is available in person in many communities, and online.

Your landlord can give you a 72-hour notice to pay or get out if your rent is more than seven days late. If your written rental agreement allows it, the landlord can give you a 144-hour notice after the fourth day that the rent is late. Like the 72-hour notice, if you have not paid by the end of the 10th day *after* the rent is due, the landlord can start a court case to evict you. Notices that are mailed to you but not posted on your door must allow for three additional days to pay.

If you pay the full rent during the notice period, the landlord must accept it. The landlord cannot require you to pay a late fee in response to this notice. The landlord does not have to accept partial rent during the notice period, or any rent after the notice period ends. If the landlord is willing to accept partial payment, the landlord may require you to sign an agreement that you will pay the rest of the rent by a certain date. If you do not pay by that date, the landlord has the right to go to court to evict you.

Rental agreement and rules violations. The landlord can give written notice that you must move for these typical reasons (and a few more not listed here):

— A one-time problem (such as a loud party);
— An ongoing problem (such as an unauthorized roommate);
— Failure to pay a late fee on a prior late rent payment;
— Pet violations;
— Violence, threats, or serious damage to the property;
— Domestic violence or stalking against another tenant;
— Extremely outrageous conduct (by you, your friends, or your pet) at or near the premises;
— Building and safety code violations not the fault of the landlord (earthquake, flood, fire damage);
— Unlawful occupancy; and
— Condominium conversion (that is, your apartment complex is being converted to condos).

For problems that the landlord says are your fault, you normally will have an "opportunity to cure"—that is, stop the behavior and save your tenancy. The amount of time you should get to cure the problem will vary depending on the type of problem. See a lawyer right away if you get this kind of notice; landlords often give the wrong kind of notice, or give it for the wrong reason. A few make up bogus reasons to retaliate against a tenant for asserting legal rights.

A-18. Eviction

Most tenants move out when they want to. But problems with paying rent, getting repairs made, and dealing with an unreasonable landlord can result in the landlord's trying to end the tenancy by taking tenants to court to evict them. Avoid this situation, because a successful eviction can cost you money, mar your credit history, and make it harder to rent in the future.

On the other hand, you may win the case in court, winning the right to keep living in your rental. Landlord-tenant law is extremely complicated, and many landlords don't always know or follow the law. If you get an eviction notice from your land-lord to terminate the tenancy, get legal advice as soon as you possibly can. By the time court papers have been filed, you should know whether you have any claims against the landlord that can help resolve the case.

A lawyer can help you determine if the landlord's notice meets the requirements of the law. If it doesn't, you may be able to get the case against you dismissed. Also, if you think the landlord is discriminating against you in violation of state or federal law, it's important to raise this issue right away. Talk not only to a law-yer in such a case, but also to the Oregon Bureau of Labor and Industries and the Oregon Fair Housing Council. See Section A-15, "Housing Discrimination," for information about illegal discrimination.

Your landlord may be retaliating against you for asserting your right to safe and decent housing. Some landlords try to evict tenants using 24-hour notices when tenants have done nothing that would allow a fast-track eviction. A landlord might have refused to accept a late rent payment during the notice period, or refused to accept a late rent payment without your paying a late fee at the same time. In short, there are many reasons that the landlord could be in the wrong.

A-19. The Court Process

The landlord can file an eviction case (also called a "forcible entry and detainer" or FED) only after giving you written notice and only after the notice period has expired. Someone will serve you with a copy of the complaint and a summons for the "first appearance." This preliminary hearing happens only a few days after you receive the court papers. If you do not attend the hearing, the court will sign a judgment allowing the police to remove you from the unit after three more days. If you attend the hearing, you can ask for more time to move out (some judges will allow you to stay for four to seven more days), or you can ask for a trial if you want to keep living in your rental and have a legal claim (defense) against the landlord's basis to evict you.

The trial will occur no later than 15 days after the first appearance; in many counties, the trial will be scheduled in just a couple of days. If you ask for a trial, you will then either fill out a court form (an "answer") listing your reasons you should not be evicted, or, if you have a lawyer, the lawyer may draft a more elaborate answer and possibly counterclaims against the landlord. There is a cost to file your answer (a "filing fee"); if your income is very low and you have few assets, you may be able to get the court to waive or at least defer your filing fee.

Before the trial, the landlord and your lawyer, if you have one, will try to negotiate a solution. In some counties, you will be asked to participate in mediation before your trial—working with a trained facilitator to help solve the issue with your landlord, without the court's imposing a judgment against either side.

If mediation is unsuccessful, at the trial the landlord will tell the court about the notice given and the reason, if any, that the landlord wants the court to evict you. The landlord may call witnesses to testify in support of the reasons. Then it is your turn to explain why you should not be evicted. The judge will make a decision immediately. If the landlord wins the case, you will be responsible for the landlord's court filing fees and other costs for the trial—and the landlord's attorney fees if the landlord had a lawyer. You can ask the judge for a little extra time to move. Otherwise, the judgment goes to the sheriff's department in about three days; the sheriff will come to your rental and remove you and your things if you have not moved out by then. If you win the case, you get to remain in your home for the foreseeable future, you may win damages stemming from the landlord's misconduct, and the landlord must pay your filing fees and attorney fees.

Even if you are evicted, be sure to take pictures of your rental before you leave, and give your former landlord a copy of your next address in case the landlord owes you back your security deposit or prepaid rent.

B.

YOUR RIGHTS AND DUTIES
AS A CONSUMER

Almost everything you buy other than for a business, or any service you use (including medical care), is subject to state and federal consumer laws. In addition, every transaction you enter into is likely to affect your ability to borrow money later and buy things on payment plans. Knowing your rights and duties as a consumer can protect you from financial abuse.

B-1. Good Credit — Getting It and Keeping It

Having "good credit" means you have a history of paying your bills in full and on time. That history makes doing business with you less risky for future lenders, insurers, landlords, employers, and credit card providers. The result is lower interest rates, lower insurance costs, and access to larger loans.

If you are just starting out on your own, you don't have a credit history yet. If you have been a tenant, had utilities in your name, used a credit card, gotten a school loan or car insurance, or have bought things on a payment plan, it's likely that your name, along with a credit score, is on file with at least one national credit reporting agency. Although each agency calculates your score a little differently, a typical score rates your creditworthiness between around 400 (terrible) to 850 (super). The scores change any time you enter into a credit transaction, and every time you make (or fail to make) a timely payment.

Lenders and sellers rely on those credit scores to decide how much they will lend you and at what interest rate. If you get behind on your bills, pay late, or don't pay your bills in full when due, your credit score will go down and stay down— for months or even years—depending on how serious the nonpayment is.

These credit reporting agencies handle billions of transactions. Not surprisingly, many credit histories contain errors—about one in four! Some of those errors can have an effect on whether you qualify for things you want or need.

You can get a free copy of your credit reports once per year to allow you to track whether the reports are accurate. (They don't all contain the same information.) You also are entitled to free reports if someone denies you credit or gives you unfavorable financing terms based on information in your credit report. The person or business that relies on the credit report must give you written notice when it makes a decision against you. You also can get free credit reports if you discover that you are the victim of identity theft and place a fraud alert on your account, if your file contains inaccurate information because of fraud, if you are on public assistance, or if you are unemployed and expect to apply for a job within 60 days.

There are two ways to get a copy of your credit reports. One is to order the reports online from www.annualcreditreport.com. Ordering online is fast, but you give up certain legal rights against the report providers by using that method. Slower but safer is to request your credit reports by calling 877-322-8228, or compete an Annual Credit Report Request Form (available from the Federal Trade Commission at www.ftc.gov and send it to):

Annual Credit Report Request Service
P.O. Box 105281
Atlanta GA 30348-5281

Errors on credit reports. Errors on your report can hurt your ability to borrow money, rent an apartment, and lots more. To correct errors, send a letter clearly explaining the problem to the credit reporting agency or agencies that have recorded the error, with a copy to the business responsible for the error. The agency and the business have 30 days in which to review the error and respond to you. If the agency agrees there is an error, it must correct or delete inaccurate, incomplete, or unverifiable information. Your letter disputing the error will remain in your credit report regardless of the outcome. If you disagree with the outcome, get legal advice about what steps to take next.

B-2. What's a Contract?

A contract is simply an agreement between parties for an exchange of promises—enforceable by law. While you are in school, you will likely sign or agree to a variety of contracts, such as a dorm room agreement, a lease for an apartment, student loan applications, a purchase agreement for a car, obtaining a credit card, or agreements for utilities or services such as cable television or Internet.

Contracts define the rights and obligations of the parties, and you should know what risks you are taking on before you sign one. Some oral contracts are legally enforceable, but it's better to get all your agreements in writing when you can. The law assumes you read the contract before you signed it. This rule includes contracts you "sign" online (unless the terms are hidden). Once you sign, you can almost never back out without remaining liable for your promise, whether or not you read the terms you agreed to. Always get a copy of any contracts you sign and keep it, in case a dispute arises later.

B-3. Heat, Lights, Water, Phone, Internet

Your utility bills can be high for lots of reasons. Old furnaces may be expensive to run; landlords or neighbors hook up power to users other than you; apartments and homes aren't properly insulated; you don't turn off lights when they're not in use; your water heater is turned up too high; you turn on the heat or air conditioning when doors or windows are left open, etc. Some students find they don't have enough money after paying rent or other necessities to pay their utility bills.

Gas, electric, telephone, and water companies can cut off service for nonpayment. They can even do it if there are children in the home. Utility shutoffs result in your having to pay a hefty deposit to get service restored. Shutoffs go on your credit report, too. (See Section B-1, "Good Credit—Getting It and Keeping It," for more information about credit reports and good credit.) You want to avoid all of these outcomes.

Avoiding a shutoff. Utility companies must follow regulations about when they can stop service. The regulations vary by type of service and type of provider. For example, heat and electricity may come from private, investor-owned companies. Some local governments operate power and water utilities. Some communities have utility cooperatives ("public utility districts" or PUDs), owned collectively by the people who use the service. All of these business models are called "public utilities," and all public utilities must have written procedures about what they must do before cutting off your service.

Public utilities must offer payment plans so that you can catch up on your overdue bills. These companies must also offer "equal pay" plans so that you pay the same amount almost every month. That is, the utility averages out your bill based on your usage over a full year. Before these utilities can shut off heat and electricity, they must give you 15 days' written notice, followed by five days' written notice, and finally an attempt to contact you on the day of the proposed shutoff. You can make payment arrangements until the final day. For landline telephone service, the company must give you only five days' written notice.

Public utilities cannot disconnect heat or electricity on Fridays, weekends, or federal holidays. Nor can they disconnect in extreme weather—on days when the National Weather Service issues a heat advisory or on days when the high temperature remains below 32 degrees.

If losing service threatens your health or safety. Special rules apply to public utility shutoffs for people with serious medical problems. The person must submit a medical certificate to the utility showing the need for the utility (for example, medicine that must be refrigerated). The person must then enter into a payment plan and pay what is owed under the plan, or risk losing service anyway.

People who are victims of certain kinds of crimes (such as stalking, domestic violence, sexual assault, or abuse of elders or those with disabilities) can keep their telephone service if they have court orders forbidding contact and may need police help. They must give the telephone company a copy of their court order and a sworn statement about the danger they face. They also must enter into a payment plan. See Section F, "Domestic Violence and Stalking," for more information.

Cell phone and Internet service plans. Contracts for cell phones and on-line phone services can be very confusing—and very expensive. Fortunately, the Oregon State Public Interest Research Group has published a guide to help you compare what you can get. Find it at http://www.ospirg.org/news/orp/tips-getting-right-cell-phone-plan. You do not have specific consumer protections from the shutoff of these services, although most of the cell phone providers offer a "customer retention" bargain price to avoid losing your business.

Ways to reduce utility costs. Most public utilities offer a "home energy assessment" to show you the biggest utility uses in your home, and then offer suggestions to reduce costs. Telephone companies participate in the Oregon Telephone Assistance Program (OTAP), which can give a discount on a basic landline or broadband service for low-income people who are eligible for some kinds of public assistance.

B-4. Buying a Car

Cars are a huge expense, both upfront and ongoing: the purchase itself, periodic registration, tires, maintenance, insurance, parking fees, repairs, and, for most car owners, gas. As a student (especially if you depend on student loans), you want to avoid the expense of having a car if you can—easy to do in Portland, Salem, and Eugene. Some transit companies offer a reduced rate for students.

For students in areas that lack good public transportation, some colleges and universities support carpooling opportunities, so check with your student government office for alternatives to car ownership.

Buying a new car. If you want to buy a new car, do your homework beforehand. First, decide what you need before going car shopping: Good mileage? Trunk space? Lots of seating? How reliable does it have to be? Does the car have to take you regularly through snow or over rough ground? (Your "must have" list should help you resist the candy-apple red convertible.)

Next, figure out what you can afford to pay. There's the purchase price, of course, but there's more. If you get financing through the car dealer or arrange for other financing, how much will each payment be? For how long? How high is the interest rate? Estimate what operating the car will cost, in fuel, repairs, insurance, and inspections. Look at Consumer Reports, Kelley Bluebook, and Edmunds web sites to learn what problems various car models have had, which cars have been recalled, etc. These three sites also can tell you what price range you should expect to see for particular models. If you are thinking about trading in a car, these sites can help you value your trade-in. You may find it more profitable to sell the old car privately. See "Selling a Used Car" below.

Most dealers are eager to finance the purchase of your new car. It's almost always better to get a bank or credit union loan with a lower interest rate, although dealers often will be willing to consider a rate lower than the one they quote first.

When financing a car, you must pay for full-coverage auto insurance before the car leaves the lot. "Full coverage" refers to collision, comprehensive, and state-mandated liability protection. Full coverage is required because when you finance the car, the loan company has a financial interest in the well-being of your vehicle: the company is the actual owner until you finish paying off the loan. Full coverage ensures that if there's an accident, the car can be restored to its pre-accident condition. Therefore, it is important to take into account the cost of the full-coverage auto insurance because it generally costs a lot more than simple liability coverage (which typically covers only the other party's vehicle repair cost and minimum medical expenses in case you are at fault in an accident).

When it's time to sign the papers at the dealership, a sales rep will try to "upsell" you—offering extended warranties and other hard-to-resist features that will raise the price of the car. Save your money: experts agree that extended warranties are usually a wasted investment. The dealer has the right to charge up to $50 to process your DMV paperwork, or $75 to process the paperwork and give you a license plate immediately.

Hate negotiating with the dealer? Feel pressured to buy? *There's no such thing as a "three day rule" that requires sellers to take back a car if you experience buyer's remorse.* If you feel outnumbered by these highly trained manipulators, you may want to look to Costco or AAA car-buying services; they may work for you.

Buying a used car. Buying a used car can be much less expensive—but also can be risky. There's usually no warranty to fall back on. How can you protect yourself from a bad choice?

After deciding which cars meet your needs and fit your budget, it's time to go shopping. Check Kelley Bluebook price ranges so you don't overpay. Now, where you should buy?

Dealers versus private sellers. Dealers run the gamut from major new-car dealerships with good-quality trade-ins with limited warranties, to street-corner auto lots with repossessed cars and cars bought cheap at auctions—and sold "as is." Cars at the street-corner auto lots are usually cheaper, but often have serious defects. If a car is running poorly and the seller tells you, "Don't worry, it just needs a tune-up," remember that a tune-up is cheap. The dealer would have given the car a tune-up if that were the only problem.

Unlike private sellers, car dealers must follow consumer protection laws, primarily disclosing the terms of the sale (and financing) in writing. Some dealers make oral promises about the quality of a car that aren't true; enforcing those promises later can be impossible.

Some car dealers try to change the terms of the loan after you have agreed in writing to the terms but before the financing comes through, making the car much more expensive. If the dealer won't give you the exact terms you agreed to, you have the right to turn in your "new" car and take back any trade-in. The dealer can charge you a reasonable amount for the short use you had of the car, and that is all.

Private sellers are more likely than car dealers to have repair and maintenance records. They usually will offer to sell at a lower price, and are less likely to pressure you into buying something you don't really want. Unlike car dealers, most private sellers want to be paid in full at the time of the sale.

Three essential protections should guide you:

1. Never buy a used car without thoroughly test-driving it.

2.   Never buy a used car without having an independent mechanic check it out thoroughly. Expect to pay from $40 to $100 for this important service, and don't buy a car from someone who won't let you have this inspection done by the mechanic of your choice.

3.   Never hand over money to a seller who doesn't have the title to the car ready to sign over to you; you may be dealing with a crook.

Selling a used car. Dealers sometimes will accept your old car as a trade-in. Most people find they get a better deal by just selling the old car themselves for cash. If you are selling a car, you definitely don't want to let go of the car before you have all of your money. You don't want any liability if the buyer gets into an accident or gets a ticket while using your car, either!

B-5. Getting Your Car Repaired

You can minimize the costs of owning a car by getting regular oil changes; that's something that you or your friends might be able to do yourselves, along with other routine maintenance. Sooner or later, though, your car is likely to need repairs. In newer cars reliant on sophisticated computer systems, not even your handy friend may have the expertise to fix the problem you are facing.

Even before you have any car problems, ask around about which mechanics are trustworthy and affordable. Check with your local Better Business Bureau and the Oregon Attorney General consumer complaints office, too, about who's trustworthy. In most cases, new car dealerships are the most expensive option for repairs; they aren't necessarily any more trustworthy than the corner mechanic, either. Check with your local community college, too. Some of these schools offer very inexpensive repairs by students supervised by skilled mechanics. Find out if the problem is under warranty for your car. And check the manufacturer's web site to see if your model of car has been recalled for the problem you are having; if so, the parts and labor might be free.

Be sure to get a written estimate of what a repair is likely to cost, and then ask other mechanics what they would charge for the same service. Ask if getting used replacement parts is a good idea, and, if so, whether the used parts will be cheap enough to make using them worth it. Also ask for the mechanic to save and give to you the parts that get replaced, in case there is any question later on about what the car needed. If you don't ask up front, the mechanic has no duty to save the parts.

Once you've decided on a mechanic, you must pay in full when the work is done unless you arrange in advance for payment over time. A mechanic who uncovers problems that go beyond the estimated amount of the work should contact you with that information and get your permission before continuing the work. Ask in advance for the mechanic to agree to do that. Honest mechanics almost always do that, but it's a good practice for you to make that advance request.

If you can't pay for the car when the work is done, and you haven't made advance arrangements with the mechanic for payment over time, the mechanic has the right to keep your car until you pay (a "mechanic's lien")—up to a point. After that time, the mechanic can take or sell the car to recover the cost of the repairs. The mechanic can file a claim for ownership with the DMV after 15 days for a vehicle worth $500 or less; 30 days for one worth between $500 up to $1,000; and 60 days for vehicles worth more than that.

What if the mechanic doesn't complete the work within the time agreed on? If the mechanic has acted reasonably to get parts or perform labor, you should agree on what seems to be a new reasonable completion date. Find out from other mechanics how long the work should normally take; if the mechanic doesn't meet the new deadline, you should try to take back your car, paying for services and parts to date. You may want to contact the Better Business Bureau or the Oregon Attorney General consumer complaints office to object, or try to mediate through one of these agencies or your community mediation program to avoid a lien when the mechanic has breached the contract to perform the work within a reasonable time.

What if the work done doesn't fix the problem? First, notify the mechanic right away to find out whether he or she will try again without charging you more. If you give the mechanic a second chance to fix the car and it still doesn't work right, you may want to take the car somewhere else to have it done right, then write a letter (keeping a copy) to the original mechanic to ask for full or partial reimbursement of your extra costs. Sometimes the Better Business Bureau or a community mediation program can help you work out the problem. You may want to file a complaint with the Oregon Attorney General's office, a step that the mechanic may not want you to take.

If you paid by credit card, you can contact the credit card company to complain and ask for it to withhold payment. However, know that the mechanic has the legal right to repossess the car pending payment. The same thing is true if you stop payment on a check; stopping payment is not free, and may result in the mechanic's filing a complaint with the police. (See Section B-9, "Checks, Credit Cards, and Debit Cards," for more information on your possible liability.)

If negotiation fails, you may end up having to file a court case against the mechanic in order to get back your car or your money or both. A claim for under $10,000 can go to small claims court (see Section H-2, "Small Claims Court," for more information). Also, get legal advice before you file a court case, because you may have consumer-law claims (such as misrepresentation about parts or service or unlawful collections efforts, etc.) in addition to your contract claim against the mechanic.

B-6. Car Tows

What should you do if your car gets towed? The answer depends on whether your car is on or next to a public roadway or in a privately owned lot.

If you leave your car next to a public road where it does not belong, a government agency, or a towing company authorized by a government agency, can tow it after 24 hours' notice. The agency can leave the notice on the car itself. If your car blocks bike lanes, impedes traffic, or creates a hazard for other vehicles, the agency can have your car towed immediately. The agency will then notify you by mail about your rights at the address that DMV has for you—a good reason to keep your driver's license address current! (Besides, the law requires you to change your license information within 30 days of getting a new address.)

If you park at a private lot, such as at an apartment or business, and your car is not permitted to be there, the owner of the lot may have your car towed—so long as all parking rules are on a sign at the parking lot. A tow operator should not monitor a parking lot unless there are signs posted in the lot that tell you what hours monitoring will occur, and cannot tow your car without signed permission from the parking lot owner. The tow operator must also take pictures of your car to show how it was parked in violation of parking rules. If you are present at the time of the tow, and the tow operator has not finished hooking up your car, the tow operator must release your car at no charge. If the hookup is complete, the tow operator may charge you a hookup fee, but not for the price of the tow.

If your car is towed from a private lot, the towing company must provide you with its phone number, the location of the car, a list of prices it will charge in order for your to retrieve your car, and the methods of acceptable payment. This information can be provided by signs posted in a parking lot, as a notice handed to you in person, or by mail if you are not present when your car is towed. You may pick up your car between 8:00 a.m. and 6:00 p.m. Monday–Friday (except holidays), and at other times within 60 minutes of requesting your car's release. You may also retrieve many of your things from your vehicle for free during business hours, even if you don't try to get your car back: prescription medication, eyeglasses, identification, a wallet or purse, credit cards, and child safety seats. The tow company can charge you only a "gate fee" if you come during non-business hours.

When you've been arrested. Police can take your car to the police station or to an impoundment lot, if they have probable cause to believe that you were driving while under the influence of intoxicants, driving with a suspended or revoked license, otherwise driving without a valid license, or driving uninsured. You will be given notice that your car was towed and what items you will need to bring to the police station or the impoundment lot in order to retrieve your vehicle. Once your car is towed, the police must take a full inventory of all the items in your vehicle, including things in the trunk. The inventory is to protect your property. The police must follow their standard procedure when inventorying your vehicle. If the police find evidence of a crime during the inventory, you may be charged with that crime.

To avoid towing problems, pay attention to where you park and how long you can park there. If you have to leave your car on a public roadway, try to pull well off the road to keep your car from being a hazard and getting towed right away. Try to get your car moved as soon as you can; towing and storage charges are hefty.

If you think your car was towed illegally, get legal advice as soon as possible.

B-7. Paying for College

Oregon established public colleges and universities to make higher education affordable. In recent years, the legislature has reduced financial support for universities, forcing the schools to push the costs onto individual students in the form of higher tuition and fees. College and university students have taken on a higher and higher debt burden. They've complained, sure, but not to their state legislators. Most students don't vote, so elected state officials aren't very responsive. If you take action, you can change that picture. See Section H-7, "Voting."

Some students or their families can pay in full for the college student's school and living expenses. And a few students get generous grants and scholarships that they don't have to pay back. But the vast majority of college students in Oregon—around 80 per cent—must rely on loans to subsidize their education if they attend school full-time. As of 2019, the average new college graduate owed around $32,000. Knowing how to borrow—and pay back—wisely can make your life after school much easier.

Student loans are available only to students who attend full-time. So colleges and universities encourage full-time attendance, because that's the best way to keep revenue flowing for the universities. It may not be the best way for individual students. For example, about 30 per cent of college freshmen drop out before the end of the school year, for a variety of reasons. If those freshmen had taken a class or two using their own money instead attending full time using a student loan, they could have walked away debt-free.

Unless there's a strong reason to finish your college program in a hurry, consider part-time studies as a reasonable alternative to taking out loans. (At some schools, taking one class doesn't even require applicants to pay an admissions fee, also saving money.) Check with your school about how long your credits stay "good"—you might have to re-take a class if several years have passed. Note: This advice comes from the perspective of saving money. If you are someone who performs better in a structured environment than with a lot of independence, as a part-time student you may find yourself with six credits five years from now. Be sure to factor in those personal variables as you decide what to do.

Obviously, if you have the choice between an expensive private college and a less expensive public institution and you'll be footing the bill yourself, it makes sense to go for the less expensive option. For example, all of Oregon's community colleges offer the lower-division courses required by state universities; tuition is much cheaper. Resist (with all your might) the temptation to attend a for-profit career school if you can get a similar program at a community college, even if the community college curriculum takes longer to finish. In most cases, the quality of the community college training is much better, at about a tenth of the cost of the private career school. Many career schools have been shut down for defrauding students.

Sources of student loan money. Banks and credit unions offer private loans for education; the federal government also makes loans, some of them based on financial need. It subsidizes need-based loans. When a loan is "subsidized," it's the government, not you, that pays the interest accruing while you are in school. Federal loans usually have lower interest rates than private loans, too, and they provide some protections for borrowers if your school goes out of business or gets shut down by the government; if you become severely disabled and unable to pay back the loan; or if you don't have enough income to pay back the loan immediately when school ends. Private lenders rarely offer these protections. Federal loans also offer a variety of repayment plans that private loans don't. See Section B-8, "Paying Back Student Loans."

Doing your student loan homework. Several online resources are very helpful to potential borrowers. One is the College Board, at www.collegeboard.org. It has a loan repayment calculator that shows how much a loan really costs over time (assuming you don't fall behind on payments, a situation that will result in additional fees as a penalty). The most comprehensive information is available from the National Consumer Law Center, with descriptions of each kind of student loan available, at www.studentloanborrowerassistance.org. Start there with "Understanding student loans" and "Repayment."

Other web sites compare different types of loans but may not have complete information about lending rates. Some of them may try to get you to sign up for help in getting scholarships. Some will urge you to consolidate loans (not necessarily a good idea)—for a fee. Stay away from web sites that charge money! All the information you need will appear on free web sites.

Living on loans. You need to know how to budget when you are living on loans. When that huge loan check comes in at the beginning of the term, it can feel like "free money." As a result, many students spend some of it on the newest smartphones and tattoos and beer and speeding tickets. That $4 designer latte you purchased with your loan money might wind up costing you $47 if you factor in the cost over time of that $4 loan money. Really. And a $47 latte doesn't taste all that great. Bottom line: Living the good life should wait until you have finished school.

When you budget, you compare your income to your expenses, and try to ensure that the expenses don't exceed what's coming in. Simple. Simple? We all know what's coming in —but we don't do a very good job of tracking what's going out. People under age 29 generally underestimate their monthly spending by a whopping 43 per cent.

Here are two exercises that can help you keep control of your borrowed money while you are in school:

1. For two weeks, write down—as you spend the money—everything you spend it on. At the end of two weeks, consider which of those items were things you needed and which were things you just wanted. Calculate the total costs for both categories. Get rid of some or all of the "wants."

2. After listing all the expenses you expect to have during school, look at the "Non-Monthly Budget List" of expenses at the end of this section of this guide. Circle all the things on that list that you didn't include

on your original list. Again, divide them into "need" and "want" categories, and say good-bye to the "wants." If you're still living in your family's home, look in closets and cabinets for things such as cleaning supplies and tools and other necessities to make sure those things are on your list, too.

When you've finished these exercises, you'll have a much better idea how to manage your borrowed money. Then make an annual—not a monthly—budget. Create your budget carefully, and limit your spending to things that you need; you will keep your spending within one or two percentage points of your income.

Non-Monthly Budget—Are These Items on Your List?

prescriptions, medical/dental

laundry detergent, bleach, dryer sheets, stain treatments, softener, etc.

car repairs

massage

property tax

laundromat

computer

dishes, glassware

passport

phone upgrades

restaurant meals

gifts (holidays, birthdays, baby or wedding showers, wedding gift)

textbooks

hunting licenses

condoms and other contraceptives

cable TV

batteries

shampoos, conditioner, brushes, etc.

ski passes

helmet

computer chargers, flash drives, etc.

pet toys, bedding

legal fees

guns, ammunition, licenses

child support

Hallowe'en costumes—yours, your kids', and your pet's

gas or diesel (car, motorcycle)

Internet access

computer repairs

pet food

furniture

concerts

dry cleaning

credit card bills

driver's license

tires

medical marijuana card

ski equipment and maintenance

toothbrushes, toothpaste, mouthwash

waxing and threading

home security system

alcohol

dish soap/dishwasher detergent

counseling

cologne, deodorant

marijuana

vitamins

jackets, coats, gloves, hats

fantasy football

insurance co-pays

work clothes

prescription glasses

renter's insurance

hair color

sunglasses

Internet account

homeowner's insurance

ski rentals

formal clothing

veterinary costs

traffic tickets

political campaigns

gym membership

recreational drugs

car insurance

hair "product"

shaving supplies

tips at restaurants/counters/gas stations

parking fees

birthday, other cards

hand lotions/creams

health insurance

oil changes

other car maintenance

federal income taxes

earbuds, headphones

child support

stationery supplies—pens, pencils,
     envelopes, stamps

bets, lottery tickets

recorded music

aspirin, ibuprofen, cough medicine, etc.

cellphone, iPhone

manicures and pedicures

party expenses

shoes

sitter—pet/children/plants/house

car loan

lessons (dance, martial arts, music, etc.)

vacations

bus, trolley fare/taxi/Uber-Lyft

chocolate, candy, popcorn

perms

vacuum cleaner

state income taxes

cycling equipment, license

jewelry

contraception

sports wear and equipment

commute costs

coffee/coffee drinks

car registration

raincoats, umbrellas

socks, stockings

broom, dustpan

duplicate keys

menstrual supplies

underwear

computer apps, programs

contact lenses, cleaners, solution, etc.

tax preparer

fed ex, shipping, etc.

charities

business licenses

bicycle, helmet, lights, etc.

pet food

Netflix, other video services

gun maintenance

boots

fraternity/sorority dues and
    social event costs

pets, purchase, licensing

sun screen

movies/films

copies

flashlights

paper

hair ties, decorations

rental application fees

photo equipment

mop, cleanser

hair cuts

church offerings

cover charges at bars, etc.

copiers, ink

range passes

casual clothing

tattoos

postage stamps

day care

books, magazines, kindle
    downloads, newspapers

B-8. Paying Back Student Loans

When you leave school—whether or not you graduate—or drop to less than a half-time course load, you must start paying back the loans you took out for tuition and living expenses. Paying back is not easy to do. Many students borrowed more than they needed, or didn't budget well, and tuition costs have increased recently, so the amount you borrowed can be quite high even if you were thrifty. In fact, only a third of all student loan borrowers are able to pay their loans in full and on time. With careful planning, though, you can craft a payment plan that will allow you to avoid penalties and negative consequences for your credit score as you begin working.

The reality check. First, figure out how much you owe to each lender. Then, set up a realistic annual budget that makes your loan payments a priority. See Section B-7, "Paying for College," for pointers. Get help from your bank or credit union, or a consumer credit counseling program.

Options for affordable repayment. Your options will depend on whether your loans are private or government loans. If your debt is from private loans only, your options are limited to what is in the contract you signed to get the loan. If the lender is willing to renegotiate the loan terms, get the new terms in writing—after making sure that you are really able to make the new payments. Unpaid private loans can go quickly to collection agencies. At some point the lender may sue you for the debt and be able to grab money from your wages or bank accounts ("garnishment"). See Section B-12, "Your Rights When You Owe Money."

If your loans are from the government, you have better options for repayment. Some people choose to consolidate their government loans, getting a much longer repayment time and smaller monthly payments, but at a higher rate of interest. (You can normally exercise this option only once, so keep it in reserve for a time when you might really need to use it.) If you have both government and private loans, some private lenders will want you to consolidate all your loans through the private lender—there's an additional fee for consolidation. By consolidating, however, you lose all of the legal rights that you once had with respect to your government loans. It's better for most people to keep their government loans and private loans separate. (If you marry and have student loan debt, there's more to consider. See Section E-8.)

Government loan borrowers' rights. When you graduate, drop below half-time student status, or withdraw from your academic program, you will have a six-month grace period before payback starts. Interest may or may not accrue, depending on your loan program.

The different government loan programs have different rules. In most cases, you are required to pay off the full loan within ten years. You usually can consolidate the loans if you need to. You can also choose from among several alternative repayment plans. These plans include getting a write-off of remaining loans after working the equivalent of ten years full-time in a public-interest nonprofit organization or in some government jobs (save proof of your employment to show you meet the requirement and make certain that the loan servicer has entered you into the right repayment plan!); a plan that starts you off making lower payments and making higher payments later on; and a "pay as you earn" plan that limits your payments to a percentage of your income. Some of the plans that write off balances after a certain period of time will result in liability for taxes on the "gift" of the money written off. Be sure to factor that possibility into your planning. Marriage can affect your payment amounts in some cases—See Section E-8.

Sometimes, you may not be able to make the required payments. In general, a borrower whose loan is overdue (delinquent) but not yet in default (up to 6 to 9 months without payments, depending on the loan) may be eligible for a deferment—that is, putting off payment. You can qualify if you are getting food stamps or other need-based financial help from a government agency, if you are temporarily seriously ill or disabled, temporarily unemployed, in the military, back in school, or in the Peace Corps, AmeriCorps, or VISTA. If the original loan was based on financial need (subsidized), no interest accrues during the deferment. You may receive up to three one-year deferments, but you must apply for them through the U.S. Department of Education in advance. Make and save records of contact you have with the DOE.

Forbearance is another way to renegotiate some government loans. Forbearance can allow you to temporarily stop payment, get more time to make payments, or get lower payments temporarily. Unlike deferment, forbearance is usually available for loans that are already in default. The lender must allow forbearance if the borrower's monthly loan debt is more than 20 per cent of income. Forbearance is not available for loans that are being collected directly by the Department of Education or other government agencies, even though the loan is a federal loan. You must make a written application for forbearance. Be careful: almost half of borrowers who get forbearance end up defaulting again within two years.

It is sometimes possible to "rehabilitate" a loan that is in default, by making nine or more full, timely consecutive payments in a row. Once you have caught up, you can choose a new payment plan, like one of the ones described above, that is more in tune with what you can pay.

At the end of this section is a glossary of student loan terminology that should be helpful to you as you determine what your rights are.

Bankruptcy is an option to discharge a student loan in only two narrow circumstances: (1) the borrower has been determined to be permanently and completely disabled and without resources to make payments; or (2) undue hardship, meaning the borrower has no ability to pay the loan in full while maintaining a minimal standard of living, and that inability will likely persist into the foreseeable future. For more information, see Section B-13, "Bankruptcy."

As of 2020, some of these repayment rights were being threatened by the U.S. Department of Education. If the law changes, you want to be sure you have the most up-to-date information possible so you can make wise decisions. The best source of information for your rights with respect to student loans is the National Consumer Law Center's student loan website at www.studentloanborrowerassistance.org. You may also want to seek individualized financial or legal advice from a financial adviser or lawyer to decide which options will work best for you. You might also contact your representatives in Congress to object to changes in the law that will harm your ability to earn a living while paying back your loans.

Student Loan Terminology

Allocation—Payments on loans are applied first to servicers for fees, then applied to interest, then to principal. (That strategy keeps the principal high even as you pay.)

Capitalization—Interest that accrues during a grace period or other deferment is added to the loan principal when repayment begins; compounding. With a subsidized federal loan, the government pays this interest as it accrues, until your grace period is over.

Consolidation—Extension of the standard repayment period from 10 years to 20 years, reducing your monthly payment amount but your increasing interest rate. Consolidation can occur only once. Consolidation is also a remedy to cure default, one time per loan, but cannot be used if the borrower's wages are being garnished. Consolidating federal and private loans together converts all the loans to private status, eliminating borrower rights specific to federal loans. It's not a step to take for the sake of convenience!

Default—After 270 days of nonpayment (or fewer for some loans), the government gains the right to garnish wages, tax refunds, and Social Security benefits. There is no time limit on collection. (Private lenders have fewer rights and fewer tools, and face statutes of limitation.) In default, the borrower loses some rights to re-negotiate loan terms and is not eligible for more loans or grants. Default can be cured by rehabilitation or consolidation.

Deferment—Extension of the grace period while the borrower is on active duty in the military, temporarily disabled, in school at least half-time, receiving need-based public assistance, unemployed or partly unemployed, in the Peace Corps, or participating in Americorps/VISTA programs. For most of these reasons, the deferment can be obtained for up to three years. An application must be made each year. On subsidized loans, the government pays the accruing interest on the deferred loans. On unsubsidized loans, interest continues to accrue and will be capitalized. A borrower cannot obtain deferment if the loan is already in default.

Delinquent—Unpaid installments on the loan make the borrower delinquent; the creditor can take no action to collect, however, until the delinquent loan goes into default.

Direct loan—a/k/a William Ford Direct Loan. The federal government makes these loans directly to students; no private lenders or guaranty agencies are involved. Direct loans are the only loans that qualify for public-service forgiveness.

Discharge—Elimination of the balance of the loan, due to the borrower's death or permanent disability. Discharge is available for direct loans and Perkins loans. The status of taxation of loan discharge is unclear at this time.

Fees—The cost associated with collecting on a defaulted loan. Fees of 20% or more can increase to as high as 40% if your account remains unpaid.

Forbearance—Temporary partial or full relief from making payments, at the discretion of the lender. All interest during a period of forbearance is capitalized.

Grace period—The time after the borrower has left school but before repayment is scheduled to start. The grace period varies according to the loan type. Interest keeps accruing during the grace period.

Graduated repayment plan—A 10-year repayment plan, with the highest payment amount no more than three times the initial payment amount, with usually three increments in payment amount over the repayment period. The initial payment rate must cover at least the amount of interest accruing between payments. (For federal consolidated loans, the graduated plan would increase the repayment period up to 30 years.)

Income-based repayment plan—Monthly payments of 10 per cent of discretionary income, revised annually, if the borrower has no outstanding federal loans since June 30, 2014 ("new borrower"); 15 per cent of discretionary income for other borrowers. The repayment period is 20 years for new borrowers, and 25 years for other borrowers.

Income-contingent repayment—Payments are 20 per cent of discretionary income for up to 25 years OR 12 years of repayment, adjusted to reflect income over time. The balance forgiven at 25 years is a taxable event.

Mandatory forbearance (a/k/a excessive debt forbearance)—The borrower is entitled to forbearance on a federal student loan when the payment required exceeds 20 per cent of the borrower's gross income.

Pay As You Earn program—The borrower pays the standard repayment amount OR 10 per cent of discretionary income, whichever is lower. The balance is forgiven after 20 years—but the amount you don't have to pay back is viewed as free money, so it's taxable. See also "revised Pay as You Earn program."

Perkins loan program—The program is administered by your participating school, and the loan is repaid to your school. A Perkins loan is need-based, and applies to both undergraduate and graduate programs. The grace period before repayment is nine months.

PLUS loan program—The borrower can be parent of a dependent student, or an independent student in professional or graduate program. Applicants must show creditworthiness. PLUS loans are not eligible for income-driven repayment plans. PLUS loans have no grace period before interest accrues. PLUS loans are subject to the borrower's right of deferment.

Public Service Forgiveness program—The balance of your loan is forgiven after 10 years for equivalent of full-time service in public and non-profit sectors (fire, police, primary and secondary teachers, social service employees, others). The borrower is responsible for proving employment records. The borrower can choose a standard payment model or payments under any of the income-driven repayment plans. Forgiveness of the balance is NOT a taxable event. Note that loan servicers have a history of putting public service loan program borrowers into the WRONG payment program, so confirm that your servicer has you in the right program.

Rehabilitation—The borrower can rehabilitate some loans to remove default status. Rehabilitation of a Perkins loan requires nine consecutive timely payments; direct loan rehabilitation requires nine timely payments in 10 months. The payments must be affordable. Collection fees are not capitalized in rehabilitation, but are attached if the borrower chooses to consolidate loans.

Revised Pay As You Earn program—The same terms as Pay As You Earn (10 per cent of discretionary income), but with a 25-year write-off for students whose loans are for graduate work.

Settlement—This offers a limited option at the lender's discretion to reduce Perkins loans. Settlement stops collection action, but does not eliminate debt. Settlement usually means that, because part of the loan will not be collected, the borrower gets that money free—so it's taxable as income.

Subsidized loan—A federal loan based on financial need of the borrower; the government pays accruing interest until the end of the borrower's grace period or deferred period.

Undue hardship—The borrower's financial status that would make it impossible for the borrower to maintain a minimum standard of living if required to make full loan payments.

Unsubsidized loan—A loan not based on financial need; the accruing interest on the loan is capitalized into the principal.

B-9. Checks, Credit Cards, and Debit Cards

While almost every seller accepts cash, many sellers also accept checks, credit cards, and debit cards, too. There are different costs—and risks—associated with each alternative to cash.

Checks. Banks and credit unions offer different types of checking accounts, including low-cost, free, and interest-bearing accounts. Some accounts have no service charges if you maintain a certain minimum balance or don't write more than a certain number of checks per month. Some "free" accounts come with checks that are quite expensive, although there's usually no extra charge for banking online. Ask about different types of accounts—and check the financial institution's fees! Some banks and credit unions offer free accounts expressly for students.

To avoid overdraft problems, keep accurate records of how much money is in your account and how much you are spending (including service fees) from that account. All financial institutions charge for NSF (not sufficient funds) checks; so do most sellers. Some sellers might take you to court for a penalty amount in addition to the original check and the bad-check charges against the seller caused by your bounced check. Information about bounced checks gets reported to credit reporting agencies, too.

Stopping payment of a check when you have a dispute with a seller is almost always a bad idea. Stopping payment is expensive because the bank or credit union will charge you for this service. Worse, intentional non-payment can be treated as a crime. Many creditors have written policies about how to resolve disputes; follow those policies. You can usually find the policies in any contract you signed with the seller. Get legal advice before stopping payment in any event— it's a step you should not take lightly.

In case someone fraudulently cashes or signs one of your checks, or creates fake checks to draw on your account, notify the financial institution and the police as soon as you find out about the problem. You will likely need to send a copy of the police report to the bank or credit union. The bank or credit union should reimburse your money, but the process could take several months.

Credit cards. Having a credit card is convenient, even though you normally must pay an annual fee to have one. A credit card gives you a record of what you've spent and where.

You've probably noticed that merchants want to lure you into using their in-house credit cards—"10 per cent off first purchase!" There are drawbacks to having more than one or two credit cards. The card can create the illusion that you have money you don't really have. Interest and late fees are steep, and card issuers aren't going to be sympathetic if you spend beyond your means. In addition, the more credit cards you have, the lower your credit score will be—even if you don't use those cards. (To get rid of all the extra cards, it's best to cancel them in writing, keeping a copy until you are sure the account really has been deactivated.)

Several federal laws protect people who use credit cards:

1. A company can't send you a credit card if you don't ask for one;
2. Every credit card statement must show how long it will take you to pay off the amount owed if you make only the minimum payment, and how much making payments will cost you in the long run;
3. Card companies must allow you at least 20 days to pay your monthly bill, and the payment must be due on the same date every month; and
4. Companies can change interest rates only after reasonable notice; they can increase interest rates in response to late payment or non-payment, but again only after notice.

Your credit card contract should contain information about your right to notice and other rights.

Save all of your credit card receipts each month and compare them with your monthly statement as soon as you receive it. If you don't recognize an entry, you should contact the credit card company immediately to question the charge. Follow up with a letter, and keep a copy of the letter. The credit card company must investigate the charge; if it appears to be an error (or fraud or identity theft), the credit card company should credit your account for the improper payment within 60 days or two billing cycles.

If you discover that an unauthorized user has stolen your credit card or credit card information, notify the credit card company as soon as you notice the theft—first by phone, then by a follow-up letter (and keep a copy of the letter). If the company gets your verbal report before the card is used, you will have no liability for any amount that the thief spends using your card. If the card has already been used by the time you report, your liability is limited to $50. File a police report, too, and send a copy of the police report to the three national credit reporting agencies and to the credit card company.

What's an "unauthorized" user? If you let someone else use your credit card for any purpose, it's almost impossible to show that the person used your account fraudulently for another purpose— unless you bothered to put that one-purpose limitation in writing. Best advice: don't let anyone else use your credit card.

Debit cards. Debit cards look just like credit cards, but they are very different. A credit card is a type of IOU, promising that you will pay later for the credit you use for purchases now. A debit card draws on money you already have, in a checking or savings account. When the money in your account runs out, your debit card will be "empty," too.

If your debit card is stolen, you may not find out until your account is completely drained. In addition, you can't withhold payment on expenses you believe are fraudulent, and your liability for charges is limited to $50 on a fraudulently used debit card only if you notify your financial institution that it was stolen or misused within two days after you find out. If you miss this two-day window, your liability could be as much as $500 for 60 days after the discovery. If you wait more than 60 days, your liability is unlimited. In most cases, your bank or credit union will reimburse your account if you notify police and the financial institution, but the process can take many months while you try to live without the money.

If you give someone else access to your debit card and that person misuses the card, you are likely to remain liable for the expenses that person incurred. Best advice: don't let anyone else use your debit card.

B-10. Identity Theft

Identity theft occurs when someone uses your identifying information without your knowledge or consent to cash in on your good name and sometimes your good credit. With your identifying information, someone might be able to write checks on your accounts, sell your things, use your credit card accounts to buy things, or get more credit cards to take out "loans."

You'll know your identity has been stolen if your checks inexplicably start bouncing, if a store rejects your debit card, if your credit-card bill is suddenly sky-high and lists purchases you didn't make, or if a collection agency contacts you to demand payment for something you didn't buy. You may be turned down for a loan you should have qualified for.

How thieves get your identifying information. Some thieves get your information simply by going through your wallet or your trash, opening your mail, or scanning your credit card. More sophisticated operations may contact credit reporting agencies, pretending to be a potential employer or landlord seeking your credit history. Some hack into big business computers or government computers to retrieve personal information. Some pretend to be charities, banks, credit card companies, or government agencies seeking to "update" your personal information. In one scam targeting students, ID thieves e-mail great news that all of the student's loans will convert to scholarships—after the student verifies a Social Security number, gives bank account information, or provides other valuable information. Some students have even been asked to submit a check (from $30 to $800) for "processing" the gift.

Avoid becoming a victim of identity theft. Minimize your risk of having your identity stolen in five ways:

1. Avoid unnecessary online transactions, such as participation in contests, taking surveys, etc. Never respond to any online request for identifying information. Lock your computer with a password to keep others from getting access to the information on it. Use a sophisticated password.

2. When shopping online, get a "virtual card" from your credit card company that gives you an alternate number good for one-time use only.

3. Receive your mail via a locking mailbox or a post office box. Never leave bill payments in an unlocked box. When you are ready to throw out old bills, first remove any identifying information such as your name and account number. Then shred the information or make it unreadable some other way. Check your bills and bank statements as soon as you get them for unusual charges or activity.

4.   Never give out identifying information over the phone. Don't agree to make charitable donations over the phone—even a $5 donation can give an ID thief enough information to drain your bank account.

5.   Keep all financial information locked up where visitors, friends, and snoops can't get it. Don't carry your Social Security card with you. Ask doctors, dentists, and other providers to delete the first 5 digits of your Social Security number from their records.

If your identity is stolen. First, file a police report and make several copies of the report. Send copies to each of the three large credit bureaus (Experian, TransUnion, and Equifax) and to the Federal Trade Commission. Notify anyone who bills you for the thief's activities that you are the victim of identity theft. Some people find they have to add fraud alerts to their credit bureau accounts and even "freeze" their credit to stop the theft, or take other steps to clear their names. Getting legal advice in this situation is important.

You should also request free copies of your credit reports from each bureau based on the identity theft. Note: It's best to do this in writing or by phone. By requesting the copies online, you waive some of your consumer rights against the credit bureaus. See Section B-1 for more information. Once you get copies, send a written challenge to any bureau that shows ID theft transactions or other errors.

When it's not really identity theft. Some people allow others to use their credit card or debit cards only to discover that the user has misused the card. Unless you have a signed a written agreement about the limits on the use of the card, misuse does not rise to the level of identity theft. It is never a good idea to authorize others to use your credit card or debit card.

B-11. Buying and Selling Online

If you're a typical shopper, you buy some of your things from a factory or store online. A couple of days later, those items show up at your door. Sometimes, however, the items don't show up, and/or your ID has been stolen, or the items were delivered but were stolen from your porch before you came home.

You may also buy or sell things on e-Bay or craigslist or similar sites, where the seller or buyer isn't affiliated with the service provider. If you either buy or sell on such a site, money needs to be transferred safely to complete the transaction.

How do you protect yourself, and your stuff, in these situations? Here are a few ideas:

1. If you're a buyer, don't order from an e-mail or text message that solicits your business. Go to the seller's web site and order from there.
2. If you're using a credit card, get an alternate credit card number for one-time use from your credit card company.
3. If you're a buyer, try to arrange for your order to be delivered to a real person so that your purchase isn't left outdoors where porch-thieves can see it.
4. If you're a seller, don't agree to accept a check in payment. It's just as easy—and safer—for the buyer to cash a valid check and pay you in cash as it is for you to cash the buyer's check.
5. If you're a seller, don't think that the buyer's cashier's check is any safer than a personal check. Even a cashier's check takes a couple of days to clear, and the buyer's money can be gone when you try to cash the check.
6. Never agree to accept payment and then forward part of the payment to a third party: this is a strategy used by sophisticated ID thieves.

B-12. Your Rights When You Owe Money

By failing to pay a debt to a person or business to whom you owe money (a "creditor"), you give the creditor the right to take steps to force you to pay, including turning over your debt to a collection agency and suing you in court for a judgment that gives the creditor the power to intercept or seize some of your wages and assets—even if you object. It doesn't matter whether you can't pay because you have lost your job, become ill, or just don't have the money. A creditor does not have to accept partial or late payments without a signed, written agreement to do so.

While being in debt can feel pretty unnerving, it's not a crime to owe money. You can't be arrested for owing money (unless you intentionally refuse to pay court-ordered child support or taxes). You have some protections against harsh collection tactics by collection agencies under federal law. In Oregon, a law called the Unlawful Debt Collection Practices Act limits the kinds of things that original creditors and collection agencies can do in their efforts to collect from you.

Is the debt legitimate? You will usually know whether you owe the money that the creditor claims you owe. But sometimes creditors, especially collection agencies, have inaccurate information. You might get a bill because the real debtor stole and used your identity. Credit reporting agencies will record these debts on your account unless they learn there is an error. A lawyer can help you untangle a wrongly recorded debt. See Section B-10, "Identity Theft," for more information.

A debt might also be invalid if the creditor waited too long to try to collect the money. This time limit, called a statute of limitation, varies from one kind of debt to another. (Time periods of three to six years are typical.) When the time period ends, the creditor loses the right to take you to court to force payment. If you make a payment then, or even agree to make a payment, you start the time period running all over again! Don't commit to pay until you know whether you still owe a debt you owed in the past. Obviously, you *can* pay if you have the money. If you can't afford to pay, though, you have no duty to take on the too-old debt.

Perhaps you co-signed a contract or loan application for a friend or relative who didn't pay—and that puts you on the hook. Or you may not recognize the name of the person or company claiming the debt; that could be because the original creditor sold the right to collect the debt to someone else, typically a collection agency. In this situation, you still owe the money if the claim is otherwise valid.

Federal fair debt collection law applies only to collection agencies. Under that law, when a collection agency wants you to pay, it must first contact you to describe the debt and any additional charges. The collection agency must then send you written notice of your right to request verification of the debt within five days of the original contact. If you orally dispute any part of the bill within 30 days, the collection agency can't assume the debt is valid. If you object in writing within that period, the collection agency must not contact you again until after providing proof of the debt. Objecting in writing is the better way to contest the debt. Be sure to keep a copy of your letter. A collector who violates this law is subject to legal penalties.

Under federal law, a collection agency can't communicate with anyone other than the debtor about the debt. "Debtor" is defined as you, your spouse, a co-signor on the debt, or your parents if you are a minor. Collectors can't contact you at work if they know that your employer forbids that kind of contact; make sure they know. You can prevent a collection agency from contacting you by notifying it in writing either that you will not pay the alleged debt or that you want no further contact from it. Be sure to keep a copy of your notice. The collection agency may file suit without violating this requirement, but it cannot continue to call or write you.

Under Oregon law, the original creditor or the collection agency can contact you at work only if it has tried to reach you at home during the day or between 6 and 9 p.m. It can then call you at work only once a week at most. The creditor or collection agency cannot call you at work at all if you tell it not to. It can write to you at work only if it has no home address for you. The collector can't use obscene or abusive language when communicating with you, and can't threaten you with arrest or jail or anything else it is not permitted to do legally. The creditor or collector can't come into your home.

When you buy something on credit, you might sign a "security agreement" that allows the seller to take back, or repossess, the item if you miss payments. This kind of agreement is typical with new and used cars, and some kinds of furniture and appliances. If you have signed this kind of agreement, the seller or collector still can't come into your home or a locked private area, or assault you or try to take the property back if you physically try to prevent the repossession. If a creditor has a court judgment against you that allows repossession, the creditor can use the police to repossess, although this rarely happens.

A creditor (including a collection agency) that has obtained a court judgment against you is known as a judgment creditor. A judgment creditor can take a percentage of your wages in a process called garnishment. The amount is usually limited to 25 per cent of your wages (higher percentages apply to debts for taxes, child support, and student loans). The judgment creditor may take all or some money from any bank account that you have. The judgment creditor may be able to force the sale of some of your possessions in order to get paid, or it may put a lien on real estate you own.

The law places strict limits on what a judgment creditor can take, however: some funds and property are "exempt" from being collected. Some types of government benefits are exempt from collection, as are basic home furnishings and clothing, some kinds of work tools and equipment, and other assets. Exemptions can be complicated; you should get legal advice as soon as possible if you receive notice that your wages or accounts or other property is being garnished. If you can show that what was taken is exempt, that property must be returned to you.

When a judgment creditor garnishes your wages or bank funds, it sends a notice, "a writ of garnishment," to your employer or bank; it must send the same notice to you on the same day. The judgment creditor must also provide you with a form to challenge the garnishment that you can file in court if you believe that the garnishment is improper or that exempt funds or property was garnished.

Once you have paid off all you owe—including interest and court fees—to the judgment creditor, the creditor must file a "satisfaction of money award" with the court to show that the debt is paid. If the creditor gets partial payments from you, the creditor should file a "partial satisfaction of money award" showing the amount paid every time until the final payment is made. See a lawyer if your judgment creditor does not notify the court that the debt is paid. And, of course, keep records of every payment you make voluntarily or that is garnished.

B-13. Bankruptcy

During their college years, many students incur large amounts of debt—in the form of student loans, cars payments, debts to landlords and utility companies, medical bills, and credit cards. Some students turn to bankruptcy in the hope of erasing these debts. Doing so makes sense in some circumstances, but it is a drastic step.

Declaring bankruptcy allows a debtor to escape from some financial obligations and to start over with a clean slate. One common type of bankruptcy, a "Chapter 7," wipes out almost all debts. Not everyone is eligible to file a Chapter 7 bankruptcy. Another bankruptcy, a "Chapter 13," provides for a three-to-five year repayment plan based on the debtor's future income that discharges some of the debt while protecting certain assets such as a home, a car, etc.

Unfortunately, declaring bankruptcy almost never allows a person to void student loans, taxes, or child or spousal support. Declaring bankruptcy has many other disadvantages. Bankruptcy can severely damage your ability to get loans and buy things on credit, long into the future. Bankruptcy stays on your credit reports for ten years. Bankruptcy isn't free, either: the debtor must pay filing fees and attorney fees. And once you have declared bankruptcy, you cannot declare bankruptcy again for eight years regardless of how high your debts become. For more information about bankruptcy and when it is available in student loan situations, see Section B-8, "Paying Back Student Loans."

C.

YOUR RIGHTS IN THE WORK PLACE

While you are in school, you may have a job or an internship. Several federal and state laws provide protections to you as an employee or an intern. You may have more rights as an employee under laws or union contracts not covered by this section.

C-1. Background Checks

The job market is very competitive. Employers want the best possible candidates they can get. Most ask for permission to conduct background checks by listing the requirement in the job posting. Background checks can include searches of criminal records, work history, driving records, and credit reports. Some employers require applicants to take drug tests. Some employers Google job candidates. Some employers even ask for access to your Facebook and other social media accounts. Smart job applicants always think about how they might look online to potential employers and references—before posting anything for the world to see, or anything that even one person might see and then circulate.

Both federal and state laws impose limits on what prospective employers can find out about you and how they can use that information. If an employer relies on a credit report compiled by a credit reporting agency to decide not to offer you a position or promotion—or if it decides to fire you based on that report—the employer must tell you so in writing, so that you can dispute any errors in the report.

In providing background check results on applicants for jobs that pay under $75,000, the credit reporting agencies are not permitted to report bankruptcies, civil suits and arrest records, paid tax liens, or collections activities. They can report criminal convictions. For higher-paying jobs, the content of the credit reports is unrestricted.

Oregon law recognizes that credit reports rarely predict whether someone will be a good employee, so Oregon law places more limits on what employers can find out. Most employers aren't allowed to use credit report information at all, but there are exceptions: federally insured banks and credit unions, employers required by federal or state law to use credit reports, most law-enforcement agencies, the state lottery commission, and the liquor control commission.

Oregon employers can't require an applicant or an employee to disclose or provide access to the person's personal social media accounts, add the employer as an authorized user of those accounts, or open the accounts in the employer's presence. An employer does have the right to look at social media accounts that the employer provides for business use.

If you think an employer or prospective employer has violated these rules, get legal advice as soon as possible. Don't forget: none of these rules prohibits prospective employers from looking at anything available to the general public, such as by Googling you.

C-2. Drug Testing for Employment

More and more employers demand that applicants pass a drug test before confirming a job offer. Marijuana can be detected in the blood for several weeks, so consider carefully whether a hit is worth it when you are searching for work. Even the use of CBD topical treatment can affect the test results. (Other drugs can be detected for varying periods of time, too.)

People who use medical marijuana to manage pain find themselves between a rock and a hard place in this situation. Until marijuana is de-criminalized at the federal level, drug testing for employment will continue to be a problem.

C-3. Starting a New Job

Once you accept a position, you may be asked to sign an employment contract or an employee handbook or manual (indicating that you have read the handbook or manual). Common terms in an employment contract include your pay rate, a description of your job duties, the length of time you will be employed, and employee benefits. Keep copies of everything that's related to your hiring, including any employment manual you receive. Also hold on to your copy of any performance evaluations you get until you have moved on to a different employer.

Some employers ask new staff to sign a non-disclosure or a non-competition agreement. A non-disclosure agreement is supposed to protect confidential information, such as trade secrets, techniques or processes, customer lists, or marketing strategies. If you disclose the employer's confidential information and another entity uses it to its own advantage, you may liable for the lost income to the employer as a result.

Using a non-competition agreement, your employer may also require you to agree not to work for a competitor in a similar position for a certain period of time. Some employers abuse these agreements, requiring them not only for staff in sensitive positions but for all staff—even restaurant workers! If you are considering part-time or temporary work and must sign a non-competition agreement in order to get the job, think twice—you may be giving up future opportunities just for a short-term paycheck.

C-4. Getting Paid

Under Oregon law, all employers must pay their employees at least the minimum wage. As of July 2020, the standard minimum wage is $12.00 per hour. In the Portland metro area, where living expenses are higher, the standard minimum wage is $13.25. In rural Oregon counties, the standard minimum wage is $11.50. The wage is adjusted to reflect inflation from time to time. The Oregon minimum wage is the same for tipped workers. There are some exceptions: outside sales people, babysitters, on-site apartment managers, seasonal employees of some educational camps, and other specific positions.

Employees must be paid for all hours worked, including preparation time, opening and closing times, and required meetings. While Oregon employers may pay by the hour, by salary, by commissions, or by piece rate, they must keep accurate time records and the employee's total earnings must at least equal minimum wage for the hours worked.

With some exceptions, employees must be paid overtime for any hours worked over 40 hours in a week. Overtime must be paid at one and one-half times the employee's regular rate of pay. Employers cannot enter into contracts with their workers to waive the overtime rate.

Most employees who work six or more hours in one work period must be given a 30-minute meal period. For four-hour work periods, employees must be paid during a 10-minute rest period. Ordinarily, employees must be relieved of all duties during a meal or rest period. Meal and rest periods may not be waived, and may not be used to adjust working hours.

Employees may be exempt from these laws if they are paid on a salary basis and are employed as executive supervisors or administrative managers, or are highly skilled or credentialed professionals.

If you believe that you have not been paid in full for hours you worked and your claim is $10,000 or less, you must file a lawsuit to get your money, hiring a lawyer or using small claims court. If your claim is greater than $10,000, you may file a wage claim with the Bureau of Labor and Industries (BOLI) online at http://www.oregon.gov/boli or by calling (971) 673-0761. You may also file a private lawsuit in court. Employers are responsible for unpaid wages for six years from the date that the wages were earned, and are responsible for two years for unpaid overtime. BOLI will not accept your wage claim if more than six months have passed since your termination date, your claim does not involve minimum wage or overtime, or more than one year has passed since the date the violation first occurred.

C-5. Unpaid Internships

Many students arrange to earn college credit in exchange for participating in a training program with an employer instead of being paid. These students serve as "externs," "practicum students," or "interns." Unpaid interns are not employees and do not have to be paid minimum wage under federal and state laws. Unpaid interns are not considered employees if they work for their own advantage at the employer's premises.

You're legally an intern rather than an employee if:

1. The training, even though it includes actual operation of the facilities of the employer, is similar to that which would be given in a vocational school;

2. The training is for the benefit of the trainees or students;

3. The trainees or students do not displace regular employees, but work under their close supervision;

4. The employer that provides the training derives no immediate advantage from the activities of the trainees or students; and on occasion its operations may actually be impeded;

5. The trainees or students are not necessarily entitled to a job at the conclusion of the training period; and

6. The employer and the trainees or students understand that the trainees or students are not entitled to wages for the time spent in training.

In addition, the employer must have a proper internship program in place that includes the following:

1. A planned program of job training and work experience for the student, appropriate to the student's abilities, which includes training related to pre-employment and employment skills to be mastered at progressively higher levels that are coordinated with learning in the school-based learning component and lead to the awarding of a skill certificate;

2. The learning experience encompasses a sequence of activities that build on one another, increasing in complexity and promoting mastery of basic skills;

3. The learning experience has been structured to expose the students to all aspects of an industry and promotes the development of broad, transferable skills; and

4. The learning experience provides for real or simulated tasks or assign-ments that push students to develop higher-order critical thinking and problem-solving skills.

If all of these components aren't in place, the employer may be obligated to pay you as an employee. Check with a lawyer before demanding wages.

Under Oregon law, even unpaid interns have certain protections. These protec-tions include having legal recourse under the state's employment discrimination laws outlined in Section C-6, "Employment Discrimination," and protection from retaliation for disclosing wrongdoing to the public or to management, known as "whistle-blowing."

C-6. Employment Discrimination

Oregon is an "at-will employment" state. This term means that, generally, an employee or intern may be fired for any legal reason. However, federal and state laws protect certain classes of employees and interns ("protected class"). Under federal law, you cannot be fired or disciplined because of your race, color, reli-gion, national origin, gender, disability, or, if you are age 40 or older, your age. In addition, Oregon law provides that you cannot be fired or disciplined because you are an injured worker or because of your sexual orientation, marital status, family relationship, an expunged juvenile record, or, if you are age 18 or older, your age. Nor can you be fired or disciplined for associating with a member of a protected class or in retaliation for opposing an unlawful employment practice under fed-eral or state law. Finally, the cities of Corvallis, Eugene, Portland, and Salem, and Benton and Multnomah counties have ordinances prohibiting discrimination. For information on the protected classes under these ordinances, contact the civil rights intake office for the city or county.

If you believe that you have experienced discrimination, try to express your con-cern with the person who has discriminated against you. If this approach doesn't work or you do not want to talk to the person directly, report the problem to your supervisor or the supervisor of the person whose conduct you think was discrim-inatory. If doing so is not possible or practical, then report the problem to the human resources department at your workplace. If your employer does not provide a satisfactory resolution, then you may file an employment discrimination claim. There are some advantages and disadvantages in deciding whether to file your claim with the state or with a federal agency, and the timelines and other procedures you need to follow, so talk to a lawyer first to determine the best way to proceed. (Note: In recent years, the federal agency has not pursued discrimination claims as aggressively as it did in the past.)

C-7. Sexual Harassment

Under federal law, an employee has a right to work free of sexual harassment because of the employee's race, color, religion, gender, nationality, age (if you are age 40 or older), genetics, or disability. In addition, Oregon law provides that you cannot be harassed because you are an injured worker or because of your sexual orientation, marital status, family relationship, or, if you are age 18 or older, your age. These laws protect both employees and interns in Oregon.

If you believe that you have been sexually harassed, you may have a claim based on any of these protected classes. Because different people are offended by different actions, an absolute legal definition is impossible. However, generally the conduct must be severely offensive to a "reasonable person", or it can be repeated moderately offensive acts that are not consensual. Such acts as occasional sexual jokes, some casual touching, or asking someone in the workplace for a date several times are not likely to be considered sexual harassment.

There are two basic types of sexual harassment:

1. Being forced to engage in sexual activity with a superior in order to keep a job, get a promotion, or receive some kind of benefit, as well as experiencing retaliation for refusing.

2. Working in a hostile environment that a reasonable person would find unbearable. Hostile environments may be created by the actions of a supervisor or a higher-ranking person, or by a co-worker or visitor to the work place.

An employer may be responsible for sexual harassment even if the victim and the perpetrator are of the same gender.

Employers must have a plan to deal with hostile environment issues and to ensure that employees know what that plan is. An employee who has been sexually harassed must follow company's rules to resolve the problem, and do what is reasonable to avoid the harassing behavior. The employer should investigate the allegation promptly.

Sexual harassment is a form of discrimination. If you believe you have experienced sexual harassment at work, you should follow the suggestions in Section C-6, "Employment Discrimination," that apply to other types of discrimination.

C-8. Rights of Workers with Disabilities

The federal Americans with Disabilities Act (ADA) and Oregon law both provide protections to employees with disabilities. These laws define disability broadly as:

1. A physical or mental impairment lasting a minimum of six months that substantially limits one or more of a person's major life activities;
2. A record of such impairment; or
3. A person's being regarded as having such an impairment, even if there is no disability.

A person is considered disabled if the limitation affects any activity that is central to daily life, even if the condition is in remission or occurs only at certain times. A person who can control a disability through medication or mechanical aids is still protected by these laws. (The need to wear glasses doesn't count.) Unpaid interns with disabilities are protected from discrimination in Oregon. Current alcohol and drug abuse are not protected under the ADA.

An employer must reasonably accommodate a disabled person so that the employee can perform the job. (An accommodation that would be a heavy financial burden to an employer is not reasonable.) The employer gets to decide how to accommodate the worker—so long as the employer's accommodation takes away the barrier to performing the work successfully.

An employer may not ask a job applicant whether the applicant has a disability. The only time a disability may be discussed is if the disabled applicant voluntarily brings it up or after a job offer is made. Any job offer may be conditioned on the applicant's being able to demonstrate the ability to perform the task successfully or passing a medical exam that verifies the applicant's ability to succeed in that position. For limits on the use of medical marijuana in the workplace to address symptoms of a disability, see Section C-2.

C-9. Retaliation

An employer cannot fire or otherwise retaliate against an employee because the employee has mentioned, asked about, or filed a wage claim. Both employees and interns are protected from retaliation for reporting or taking legal action to address any discrimination they have experienced. Furthermore, under Oregon's whistleblowing law, an employer may not retaliate against an employee or intern for reporting employer misconduct.

C-10. Personnel Records

If an employee or intern asks to review his or her personnel records, the employer must provide reasonable opportunity within 45 days for the employee or intern to inspect those records of the employee or intern that have been used to determine the employee or intern's qualifications for hiring, promotion, pay increases, employment termination, or other disciplinary action. Employees or interns may also ask the employer or former employer to make copies of their personnel records for a reasonable copying charge. If you sense that your job situation is changing for the worse, it's a good time to review your personnel file to verify that positive reports from past evaluations, etc., are still in it.

C-11. Social Media and Privacy at Work

Oregon law prohibits your employer or prospective employer from asking for your passwords or for access to your social media accounts, or from requiring a co-worker who can view information posted to those accounts from sharing that information with your employer. Under the Stored Communications Act, your employer would also likely be prohibited from using any passwords you might have stored on your computer to access your accounts. However, if your social media profile is available to the public, an employer may be able to use the information to take disciplinary action against you. As a general rule, don't post information on your social media site that you would not want your employer to see.

Your employer can access information stored on a computer, telephone, tablet, or other device provided by the employer for work purposes. Your employer can search your workspace, including your desk if it is in an open, easily accessible area. However, your employer generally can't search your personal belongings, such as a purse or backpack.

D.

SEX AND THE LAW

Your privacy rights cover your sex life. At the same time, criminal law applies to some kinds of sexual conduct, so you should know what the limits are.

D-1. Consensual Sex

When adults willingly have sex, their conduct is said to be consensual. This kind of sexual activity is legal, regardless of the gender of the adults—so long as nobody gets hurt. (For more information about same-sex relationships, see Section H-4, "LGBTQ Issues.")

Consent is an informed, voluntary, and sober agreement. If you are too drunk or too drugged to make decisions, you cannot consent. Forced "consent" is not consent.

Consent isn't a one-time conversation, either. If you want greater sexual intimacy, you must ask, every time. Even if you are in a relationship, you cannot assume that you have permission to have sex with your partner. Silence or the absence of "no" does not mean "yes."

D-2. Pregnancy

Oops! Just under half of all pregnancies are surprises. And when you're trying to make it through college, pregnancy isn't necessarily a good surprise.

Your partner may have told you, "Don't worry, I've taken care of it"— when your partner hasn't taken any precautions at all against getting pregnant.

People get pregnant for all kinds of reasons, many of them not so good for future children: to pressure someone to marry them, to humiliate their parents, to have an attention-getting trophy, to appear "adult", to guarantee that someone (the child) will love them. Experts suggest that a much better motive for making a baby is to offer a child a safe and stable home.

There are also people who think that making someone pregnant will give them control over that person. This is not a romantic impulse, and those people will become more obviously abusive as time goes by.

If you're pregnant and you want to end the pregnancy, talk to campus health services or another provider. You can also get "morning-after" and other contraceptives without a doctor's prescription from most pharmacies in Oregon. Going through with the pregnancy is another option, as is adoption.

You can't force the other person to have a baby OR have an abortion. If your long-time partner or your one-night hookup opts for a baby, it's time for you to talk to a lawyer about custody and child support.

The take-away here is that you can't rely on your partner to be on the same page you are. If you want to avoid a pregnancy, take full responsibility—every time— for protected sex.

D-3. Sexual Assault

Sexual assault is any unwanted sexual contact. It can range from violent rape to annoying inappropriate touching. It can be a crime and it can be a "tort" (in a lawsuit for money damages). A person convicted of sexual assault may have to register as a sex offender when released from prison.

If you are the victim of rape or other severe sexual assault, your first impulse is likely to take a shower and wash or throw away your clothes. A better course of action is not to do those things—you'll be getting rid of critical evidence if you decide at some point to press charges against your assailant. Instead, go to the nearest emergency room to make sure you are okay, and to get emergency contraception and preserve evidence. Domestic violence and rape intervention advocates affiliated with a local women's shelter can help you through that experience.

You do not need to file charges against the attacker, or even talk to the police, in order to get these important hospital services. You also can seek more help from domestic violence intervention advocates. Find contact information in Appendix I, "Getting Help."

Many advocates recommend filing charges, difficult as that may be, because sex criminals will likely continue their abuse until they are stopped. If you file charges, you also may be eligible for crime victim compensation (see Section G-9, "Crime Victim's Rights," for more information).

If the sexual assault (or harassment or stalking) occurred on campus, you can report it to campus security. You can report on campus even if you are just a witness to that crime or stalking, harassment, or any other form of sexual abuse. Most colleges and universities must take steps to protect victims, witnesses, and others from retaliation for reporting acts of sexual assault. Colleges also must have a policy to address immediate threats to the health or safety of students or employees on campus.

D-4. Help from the Court

Whether or not you report a sexual assault to the police, you may remain concerned for your safety from further attack by your assailant. Oregon law offers a sexual abuse protective order (SAPO) in some situations to prohibit your assailant from contacting you. For adults in certain kinds of relationships, a protection order under the Family Abuse Protection Act (a "FAPA order") is what you need. See Section F, "Domestic Violence and Stalking."

A FAPA order can prohibit contact if your assailant is:

—   An adult with whom you've had a consensual sexual relationship in the last two years;

—   Your spouse or domestic partner or former spouse or domestic partner;
—   Someone with whom you've lived in an intimate relationship;
—   The other parent of your child; or
—   Related to you by blood, marriage, or adoption.

If your attacker is none of these, you likely qualify for a SAPO.

Your assailant must have been an adult at the time of the assault. If you already have a civil or criminal no-contact order against your attacker in Oregon or any other state, that order should be all you need. Call police if there is any violation of the restrictions in the order.

SAPOs are free; the court provides application forms. Fill out the application carefully and truthfully. You can keep personal information such as your address and telephone number from appearing in the court record; the court clerk will explain how. A copy of the order is delivered to your assailant, who has 30 days in which to challenge the order by requesting a hearing. It's important to confer with an advocate, including a lawyer, when applying for the SAPO and, especially, if your assailant asks for a hearing. You must attend the hearing.

D-5. Sexually Transmitted Infections

Partners can transmit diseases to one another through unprotected sexual relations. Some sexually transmitted infections (STIs) are fatal or permanently disabling. Some make you sterile. All carry stigma and discourage others from becoming your partner.

Negligently or intentionally transmitting an STI can result in a costly and public lawsuit from someone you infect, or even criminal prosecution for a felony, including attempted murder or homicide, for knowingly passing on an STI.

Take sensible precautions to ensure safe sex. And if you have or might have an STI yourself, always disclose that information to a potential partner—beforehand.

D-6. Sexually Explicit Communication

Photo and video recording features are common on telephones, tablets, computers, and other devices. Never (never, never ever) share sexually explicit photos or videos with anyone, even someone you think you can trust. So many "trustworthy" people with intimate pictures have circulated them that there's even a state law now to try to limit the damage they've done.

Photos and videos that are published online on social media sites and other web sites can be very difficult to remove or control once online. They can be printed out and circulated, too. This activity is sometimes termed "revenge porn."

Former partners who want to punish you (for discovering what jerks they are?) aren't the only people who distribute private images. Strangers hack into devices looking for photos and videos that they can sell.

It's a misdemeanor to circulate any image showing genitals or women's breasts without consent if the person in the image is recognizable. If the conduct is repeated after successful prosecution, it becomes a felony. In addition, the victim of this crime can file a civil suit that can result in a minimum of $5,000 in damages. A person who has distributed the images for money must pay the victim the full amount of the profit.

E.

PARENTS, CHILDREN, AND THE LAW

As the college student population becomes more diverse, it is more common than ever for students to be married or in a committed relationship, to be divorced or separated, or to have children—even by surrogate or artificial insemination. The law with respect to your status in a family or relationship is extensive and important to know.

E-1. Parentage and Child Support

If you are a man who has impregnated a woman (not as an artificial inseminator/ sperm donor), you have no legal right to stop her from bearing the child. This rule applies whether or not you are married to the pregnant woman. Once the child is born, you can acknowledge that you are the father (it's usually presumed you are the father if you are married), or you can ask for a paternity test so you can be sure.

If a paternity test shows that you are the father, you can expect that the mother, if she wants custody of the child, will seek child support. If you are in a same-sex marriage, the law presumes you are both financially responsible for the children you have while married, so the child support rules will apply to you, too. (See Section E-2, "Custody of Minor Children," for more information.) Note that either parent can request custody. In Oregon, child support is based on a formula that takes into account the incomes and normal living expenses of both parents. It also factors in such things as health insurance and medical and dental care for the child, and how much time the child spends with each parent.

The law rarely takes into account whether either parent is going to college. Instead, the law presumes that, unless you are severely disabled or in prison, you have the ability to earn at least minimum wage at a full-time job. For some parents, that rule may mean that you must leave school in order to meet your child support obligations. See a lawyer about your duties and the choices you can make—before signing court papers or a birth certificate making you liable.

Most parents pay child support through automatic withholding of a part of their paychecks; the state then distributes the money to the parent receiving support. Some payers arrange to make payments in other ways, but the state provides the best record for both parents of what was and wasn't paid.

If a parent paying state-mandated child support gives the child gifts or gives extra cash to the other parent, these gifts are not credited against child support that's required to be paid in the future. After a child support amount is set, either parent can ask for it to be changed if there is a substantial change in the circumstances of either one of them.

The state may garnish (take) some of the wages and bank accounts or state and federal tax refunds of parents who fall behind on their child support payments.

E-2. Custody of Minor Children

Married or not, people who have children together have equal rights and duties with respect to those children until a court says they do not. The court's decision could come in a divorce case or, if the parents are unmarried, in a custody case.

The court makes its decision based on what is in the best interests of the child; either parent could be awarded custody under that standard. The court treats same-sex married couples the same way. The court will establish how much parenting time each parent will have, and when; how much child support should be paid; and how the parents will share the costs of health insurance and medical care for the children. In most Oregon communities, parents can work with a family court mediator to create their own parenting plan to address those questions, and then present their plan to a judge for signature. As the children get older, the parents may want to look at their plan and adjust it to meet the children's changing needs.

If the parents agree, they may share joint legal custody of their children, in which both parents are responsible for making certain decisions for their children. If the parents do not agree to joint custody, the court must award sole custody to one parent or the other.

E-3. When Others Provide Care for Your Kids

Students who are parents may need help from babysitters, day care providers, and after-school care providers (including friends or relatives). Make sure that all of these people know how to reach you, your child's doctor, and your child's dentist. Make sure to give these people a list of allergies and medicines for your child, and your child's health insurance information. People other than parents can authorize only emergency care, so if you want caregivers to be able to authorize routine medical or dental care, you'll need to give them your written permission.

E-4. Child Care for Extended Periods

Relatives or friends may care for your child for weeks or months while you are in school. In that situation, the caregivers may need to demonstrate to schools, as well as to health care providers, that they have authority to make decisions for your child. Oregon has a special power of attorney for the care of minor children that can be valid for up to six months (longer if a parent is on active military duty). School districts and medical providers in Oregon must honor this temporary power. You can create a new form for additional six-month periods. For a sample form for this purpose, Protect Your Family - Family Emergency Preparedness at https://oregonlawhelp.org/issues/family/family-law.

E-5. The Rights of Grandparents

Many children have good relationships with their grandparents, and many parents are grateful for grandparents' involvement. For those families, the questions about grandparents' rights never come up.

Sometimes, however, there is conflict between a child's parents and grandparents, and the child's grandparents demand access to the child. The law presumes that parents act in the best interests of their children. There is no such presumption related to grandparents. In Oregon, a grandparent must prove that it is in the children's best interests to spend time with the grandparent if that grandparent wants to establish an enforceable schedule and relationship with grandchildren. The grandparent must file a court case for that purpose, and must give formal notice to the parents. Parents have the right to object in court.

E-6. Protecting Your Child's Safety, and Your Own

You may have temporary or permanent legal custody of your child as the result of a court order. Anyone you authorize to take care of your child—including your child's day care, school, and other caregivers—should have a copy of any current court order relating to your child.

What if someone who is court-forbidden from contact with your child—an abuser—tries to see your child? Make sure that your authorized caregivers know what to do (call the police!) if the person restricted from seeing the child tries to contact or even take the child when the child is with others.

Both parents of a child are normally entitled to see the child's school records. An abuser may seek the records in order to discover where the other parent is living or to attempt to abduct the child. A federal law can keep a school from disclosing those records if a court orders the school not to disclose. Ask a lawyer about getting that protection if you are concerned about your safety or your child's safety. See also Section F, "Domestic Violence and Stalking."

E-7. Living Together

Unmarried persons often live together as a couple. In most circumstances, they have no rights over each other in this unmarried arrangement. If the unmarried couple incurs debts together (buying a house or entering into other types of contracts they both sign), they will both be liable for those obligations. Things they buy separately will remain the property of the individual purchaser. Legal problems can arise when one person has signed a contract for a purchase but both people contribute funds to the purchase. Likewise, if one person works to support the other person while the other person attends school or gets professional training, the supporting person may have a claim for partial or full reimbursement later on. When it comes to financial arrangements, partners should get legal advice about how to protect their separate interests.

People who live together usually find it necessary to authorize doctors and hospitals in writing to give information to their partners about their medical conditions and treatment; otherwise, health care providers cannot share that information without violating federal law.

E-8. Marriage

In Oregon, any competent person age 18 or over is eligible to marry someone else of any sex who is competent and age 18 or over, unless they are first cousins by blood.

People who plan to marry must obtain a license to do so, and must participate in a formal ceremony overseen by a judge, a justice of the peace, a county clerk, or a clergy member, before two witnesses. Oregon does not authorize "common law" marriage, although people who are lawfully married under the common-law rules of another state are considered married when they are in Oregon.

A divorce from an earlier marriage must be completely final before a person can marry again.

Marriage makes both spouses liable for "family expenses" of the other—including everything from home improvements to each other's medical care, and student loans they incur once they are married.

A spouse is not responsible financially for debts incurred by the other spouse before marriage.

For those with student loans incurred before marriage, there are some important things to consider:

1. The debt you bring into the marriage can impair your ability to buy a home or support children. Both partners should commit to a financial plan to address their student loan debt.
2. The type of loan repayment plan you choose can be affected by marriage. If you have an income-driven repayment plan for federal loans, and you file taxes as "married filing jointly," your spouse's income will be considered as yours—and your payment obligation could go up dramatically. See a tax specialist about how to approach your situation.
3. Some private loans do not discharge the debt if the borrower dies. The surviving spouse could become responsible for it. (Federal student loans discharge the debt in this situation.)
4. If you choose marriage as a time to consolidate your loans (see Section B-8, "Paying Back Student Loans," for information about whether consolidation is a good idea), be aware that you can't combine your federal loans with your spouse's federal loans. A few private lenders will consolidate loans for spouses.

E-9. Step-Parenting and Adoption

A person who marries someone with a minor child becomes a step-parent. A step-parent has no legal rights over the child during the marriage. For example, without written authorization from the child's parent, a step-parent can't register the child for school or take the child to the doctor for non-emergency care. But a step-parent has a duty to provide basic support for the child during the marriage (even if the child's other parent pays child support).

A step-parent can adopt a step-child with the consent of the parent and the absent parent, or without consent of the absent parent who has paid no support, has never lived with the child, or has a long-term incapacity. If the child is age 14 or older, the child must consent to his or her adoption by a step-parent before a court will allow the adoption. Even if the step-parent has not adopted the child, if the parent and the step-parent later divorce, the step-parent may be able to obtain parenting time with the child by persuading a judge that it's in the child's best interest to spend time with the step-parent.

E-10. Divorce and Legal Separation

Spouses with "irreconcilable differences" that result in the breakdown of their marriage may divorce in Oregon. If, for religious or other reasons, spouses cannot divorce, the spouses can legally separate through court proceedings. Just living apart is not the same as a divorce or a legal separation.

When spouses divorce ("dissolve their marriage") in Oregon, they—or a judge, if they can't decide themselves—must determine how to divide their property and their debts, how to divide time with their children, and how much child support should be. One spouse may want spousal support. In most counties, the couple can meet with a family court mediator to try to work out these questions.

Oregon is not a community property state. Therefore, the court's job is to make sure that property the couple obtained and debts they incurred in Oregon are divided "equitably," which may be but is not necessarily "equally."

A spouse's liability for new debts incurred by the other spouse ends once they have physically separated, in anticipation of divorce, for the last time. Document when you began living separately; you should notify creditors that, from now on, you are not responsible for the debts of the other person. You should get separate bank accounts with a you-only debit card, cancel joint credit cards, and get credit cards in your name only. See Section B-12, "Your Rights When You Owe Money," for more information.

People who have few possessions and few debts can get a divorce faster by filing as co-petitioners. Whether or not a couple qualifies for the co-petition method, if the spouses agree about how they want to address all of the financial, custody, and support issues, one spouse can file a petition for dissolution and the other spouse can allow the case to go through "by default"—that is, without filing any papers or appearing in court because he or she does not contest anything that the filing spouse laid out in the petition.

Note: It is not possible to get a default divorce from someone who is on active duty in the military. Get legal advice about how to proceed in this situation.

It's a good idea to get legal advice when divorcing, even if you think you will agree on the terms: there may be issues you don't know you have to address, and some decisions have big tax consequences that you should know about beforehand.

F.

DOMESTIC VIOLENCE AND STALKING

Partner abuse, or domestic violence, is unfortunately quite common. About 90 per cent of domestic violence is perpetrated against women. But regardless of gender, domestic violence violates the law. On most campuses, students have access to confidential counseling services from women's resource centers and similar groups if they are concerned about discomfort and fear in a relationship.

In Oregon, domestic violence is defined very broadly. It covers violence between people who do or did live together, relatives, people who have a child together, and people who have or had a sexual relationship. (Sexual assault on someone not in these categories is addressed in Section D-3, "Sexual Assault.")

Domestic violence includes obvious things like hitting, shoving, choking, sexual assault—things for which police can arrest and the state can prosecute the offender in a criminal case. Domestic violence also includes constant surveillance (including message tracking and GPS surveillance), belittling and humiliating, isolating the victim from family and friends, harassment at work or at school—things that may or may not fall into the category of crimes but that can be personally devastating.

Offenders typically blame alcohol or drug consumption—or the failings of the victim—for their behavior. Those who engage in this kind of violence frequently harm the victim's children as well. Domestic violence tends to worsen over time, some-times ending in the death of the victim and even the victim's children and pets.

State law offers some protections against future violence, and support groups and shelter programs provide resources for those who want to escape the violence. Get as much information as you can so you can decide what works for you. See Appendix I, "Getting Help," for more information.

If the police make an arrest, the district attorney may file criminal charges against the abuser. You may be called as a witness. The district attorney's victims' assistance office can help you prepare for the hearing, protect confidential information, including your address, create a victim impact statement to be used in sentencing, request release and probation terms that order the abuser to stay away from you or not be allowed to have guns, and apply for crime victim compensation funds in some cases.

Even if the police and the district attorney have not been involved, you can still take steps to protect yourself in a civil (non-criminal) court case. You may qualify for a protection order under Oregon's Family Abuse Protection Act (a "FAPA order"), including an emergency temporary order on weekends with help from police. You can get an order free and without a lawyer. Signed by a judge, the order requires the abuser to stay away from you; the order also may require the abuser to stay away from your children or other family members or your household. The order may be able to force an abuser living with you to move out, or to give up weapons. A person who violates the order must be arrested.

A FAPA order is available to you if you have been abused within the last six months and believe you are in danger of further abuse from a spouse, a former spouse, the other parent of your child, an adult related by blood, adoption, or marriage, someone you lived with as a partner, or someone with whom you were sexually intimate in the last two years. (See Section D-4, "Help from the Court," for a sexual-assault protection order if you are the victim of a sexual assault and not in one of these categories.)

The abuser gets notice of the FAPA order after a judge signs it, and the law allows the abuser to request a hearing about your claim. You will get notice from the court about the hearing date and time. Get legal help if at all possible, and talk with a victims' advocate about your safety when arriving at and leaving from the courthouse.

In a divorce or custody case, a judge can include protection orders for you and your children based on the conduct of your abuser. At your request, the judge can allow you and your children to move more than 60 miles further away from the other parent without giving advance notice. The judge also can order that your personal information, such as your address, place of work, telephone number, driver's license, etc., be kept out of the public records. You also can ask for protection of your child's school records so that your abuser doesn't find out where you live from those records.

If you suffered pain, had medical expenses, or needed to move as the result of the conduct of any abuser, you may be able to file a lawsuit against that person for damages (money). There is usually a two-year limitation on this kind of lawsuit; talk to a lawyer who can help you evaluate your case.

You can apply for child support from the other parent without necessarily disclosing personal information. When you apply, fill out a "claim of risk." You will want to obtain an "address of record" where you can get correspondence but where you do not actually live; ask the child support worker or a domestic violence program how to obtain an address of record.

Oregon law prohibits landlords from discriminating against applicants and tenants because they have been victims of domestic violence, sexual assault, or stalking. The law also allows tenants in these situations to get out of leases if they need to move for their own safety; permits landlords to remove an abuser from the rental agreement and evict that person; and lets tenants change the locks at their rentals to stay safer. For more information about your rights as a tenant in this situation, see Section A-16, "When You Want to Move Out," and Section A-17, "When Your Landlord Wants You to Move Out."

You may want to see a lawyer if:

— You sense that your landlord or prospective landlord is treating you differently from the way the landlord treats other tenants;

— Your landlord won't let you break your lease or rental agreement without a penalty after you have been a victim of domestic violence, sexual assault, or stalking, and you have given 14 days' written notice of termination of the tenancy along with a copy of a civil protection order, a police report, or a written statement from a police officer, an attorney, a licensed health care professional, or a victims' advocate; or

— Your landlord won't change your door locks at your expense after a co-tenant who abused you has been ordered by a court to move out. (You must have a Family Abuse Protection Act order signed by a judge in order to qualify for the change of locks, and you must have shown a copy of it to the landlord.)

A stalking protective order can help protect you, your immediate family and other members of your household, from someone—including a complete stranger—who has, on at least two occasions in the past two years, put you in reasonable fear for your physical safety. Conduct can include watching you, waiting for you, following you, sending presents, threatening you, and contacting you against your wishes. You can petition for a stalking protective order from a judge or from a police officer. A hearing is involved; the stalker has to show why the stalking protective order should *not* be entered.

G.

CRIME AND CRIMINAL RECORDS

This guide looks at some of the most common criminal-law problems that college students encounter. (See also Section D-3, "Sexual Assault," for more information about the crime of sexual assault, Section F, "Domestic Violence and Stalking", and Section H-1, "'Greek' Life," for more information about hazing by fraternities and other student organizations.)

Some of these problems are potentially felonies punishable by more than a year in state prison, substantial fines, financial restitution, and community service. Among other things, a felony conviction can keep you from qualifying for government-subsidized student loans in the future and from getting many kinds of jobs. And stiff fines and court costs that you don't pay immediately will seriously damage your credit. ("Immediately" means on the same day the judge announces the fines and costs, or your bill will go to a collection agency, at a higher cost.) You may be required to attend a treatment program at your expense, and your driver's license may be suspended for driving-related offenses.

All of these problems cause stress and uncertainty, and dealing with them can cost thousands of dollars. Read this section of this guide to learn how to avoid these problems.

G-1. Dealing with the Police

As a college student, you may interact with campus security or local and state police. Both you and the police have certain rights when you have contact; those rights vary depending on the circumstances. The distinctions are important:

— The police may simply be seeking general information;
— they may "stop" you to check you out because they suspect you are committing or are about to commit a crime; or
— they may have a reasonable belief (probable cause to believe) that you have committed or are committing a crime or a violation, in which case they may cite you or arrest you.

Police who are seeking general information can approach you to ask questions. You have no duty to answer questions. If you want the police to stop talking to you, always ask if you are free to leave before leaving. Never run from police, and never leave when the police have ordered you to stop. Doing so may be a crime—and dangerous.

In Oregon, you have no duty to tell the police your identity. (If you are driving, of course, you must show that you are licensed to drive.) You do not have to give the police your Social Security number. If you are not a U.S. citizen and you are stopped or arrested, you must show your international student identity card. It is a crime for anyone to provide false identifying information. See Section H-6, "International Students", for more information about police encounters.

If the police tell you that you are not free to leave, or, if they've pulled your car over and they have your driver's license, you are not free to leave. You are "stopped" or detained. Police can't detain you without reasonable suspicion that you committed, are committing, or are about to commit a crime. In Oregon, if the police have stopped you with reasonable suspicion about one crime, they cannot ask you questions about any other crimes while you are not free to leave. Once they tell you that you can leave, hand you a traffic ticket, give your license back— all signs that you are free to leave— the "stop" is over and they can ask about anything they want. Once more, you have no duty to answer questions.

Police may ask if they can search you or your belongings. You do not have to agree to let them do so. You should say simply and politely that you do not consent. If the police threaten to get a warrant in order to search, you can insist that they get one: the police can't get a search warrant without a good reason. They may be able to detain (stop) you until they obtain a warrant. If the police insist on searching without a warrant, do not resist and do not argue. Simply repeat politely that you do not consent to a search.

If police who have stopped you reasonably suspect that you have a weapon, and they reasonably suspect you might be dangerous, they have the right to pat down your outer clothing solely for the purpose of finding the weapon. They do not need your permission to do this. It's a good idea to tell the police if you do have a weapon, so they don't overreact if they find one.

When dealing with the police, be courteous and cooperative at all times. Even if you think there's no reason for them to detain you or search you or arrest you, it is a crime to resist arrest. Some police have a fairly elastic definition of "resist." Only a court can decide whether the arrest was lawful in your case. You can always ask the police for their names and badge numbers or their business cards. Remember that anything you say to the police, no matter how harmless it seems at the time, can be used against you if you are arrested. It is best to say nothing. Second best? If you can't resist talking, don't lie. (Lawyers routinely advise their clients never to talk to the police about anything that has happened and to insist that they be able to see a lawyer. Once you have asked for a lawyer, all questioning by the police must stop.)

You can't be arrested for a violation, such as a speeding ticket. The police can issue you a citation to appear in court on such charges. Make sure you show up at the date and time listed on the citation.

If the police arrest you, they take you under their control so you can be charged with a crime. Oregon allows arrests for felonies (punishable by more than a year in prison) or misdemeanors (up to a year in jail). In addition to (or instead of) imprisonment, you may face fines, court costs, conditions of probation, and other penalties. You also can be arrested if there is a warrant outstanding for your arrest—for such things as probation violations or failing to appear in court in a criminal case or in response to a traffic or parking ticket when you haven't paid the fine. Failing to appear is a crime in itself.

The police do not have to tell you why they have arrested you. They do not have to read you your constitutional rights—a "Miranda" warning—when they arrest you. The police must give you that warning only if you are in their custody AND they are questioning you as a suspect.

You have three constitutional rights if the police arrest you:

1. You do not have to talk to the police. You have the right to remain silent. If you do talk, the police can use what you say as evidence in a prosecution against you.
2. You have the right to talk to a lawyer before deciding whether to answer any questions.
3. If you can't afford a lawyer, the court may appoint a lawyer for you.

If you are arrested, you are taken to a police station to be "booked." Staff will photograph you and take your fingerprints. They will inventory your belongings for safekeeping and give you a receipt for them. If they find illegal drugs or weapons, or evidence of a crime, during this inventory, the police are allowed to use that information as evidence against you. You are allowed to make a telephone call to a lawyer or other person to get help in getting released.

You may be released immediately or be held in jail until a hearing, where your lawyer can represent you or the judge appoints a lawyer, and enter a plea of guilty or not guilty. At this hearing, the judge will decide whether you must post bail (money) in order to be released until trial. In very serious cases, the judge can refuse to release you.

G-2. Alcohol and Drugs

Sound like a recipe for a good time? Maybe. But alcohol and drugs are certainly the recipe for trouble. About 80 per cent of people who get arrested are under the influence of alcohol or drugs at the time they commit the crime.

Typical kinds of trouble for college students include things like speeding; drunk driving; possessing alcohol when under age 21; using fake identification to buy liquor or marijuana; public drunkenness or offensive littering; or using, possessing, or distributing illegal drugs.

A person under age 21 may not try to purchase or acquire alcoholic beverages anywhere but in a private home in the presence of a parent or guardian or with a parent or guardian's consent. Nor may a person under age 21 enter a bar or club that prohibits minors.

Marijuana use by those over 21 for "recreation" is now legal in Oregon—but only under state law. Under federal law, possessing small amounts of marijuana is still a crime. State and local police will not arrest a user for this federal crime. "Medical marijuana" has been legal in Oregon for quite a while. It allows a person with medical certification to grow a small number of plants, as well as purchase and use marijuana. Federal law does not recognize medical marijuana as legal, either.

Both types of marijuana users—recreational and medical—are likely to have out-of-state friends who want some high-end marijuana sent or delivered to them. Bad idea. As soon as you cross the state line with your package, Oregon law doesn't protect you any more. Another state's law will apply. And if you fly with marijuana or put it in the mail or FedEx it, your conduct is now subject to federal law and thus is a crime.

Possession, use, and distribution of other so-called controlled substances—such as heroin, cocaine, ecstasy, LSD, methamphetamines, PCP, and other hallucinogens, and even prescription drugs if they're not yours—are felonies under both state and federal law. If you live with others who have illegal drugs in your home and those people are arrested, you may be arrested, too.

G-3. Driving Under the Influence of Intoxicants

Driving when drinking or using drugs has potentially severe consequences, both legal and real-life. Drivers under the influence can kill or maim others, and end up themselves disabled, wheelchair-bound, and paralyzed. As for the legal consequence, in Oregon you can be convicted of driving while under the influence of intoxicants (DUII) if you drive when you are affected by liquor, a controlled substance, or an inhalant in a public place. If convicted, you'll be fined $1,000, and your driver's license will be suspended for one year, three years, or permanently, depending on whether you have been convicted of DUII before.

How do the police know if your driving is impaired? There are three ways. The first way is the police watch the way you are driving: it looks "off." The second way is called a "field sobriety test," in which the police examine your ability to track things visually, ask you to perform certain functions such as walking in a straight line or counting, reacting to moving light, etc. The third way is that, in exchange for getting your driver's license, you agreed to a breath, blood, or urine test if the police ask for it. If you are over age 21, you will fail the test if the volume of alcohol in your blood is .08% or more. If you are under age 21, you will fail the test if there is *any* amount of alcohol in your blood. You may refuse to take the test, but your refusal will be used in court.

If the state intends to suspend your driver's license, it will send you a notice; you are entitled to a DMV hearing to see if you can keep your license. (The hearing is separate from the criminal trial.) You do not have to ask for the hearing, but if you want one, you must ask for it within the time period in the notice. You likely will need help from a lawyer.

If you are charged with DUII for the first time, you may be eligible for a diversion program that would keep you from getting a conviction on your record. You must do all the steps of the program to avoid conviction. You have to pay for the program. You also have to install and use an Ignition Interlock Device (a breath analyzer) in any car you drive—also at your expense.

If your license is suspended for a DUII conviction, you must complete a lengthy court-ordered treatment program at your expense. You must provide proof to the DMV that you have a completed the treatment program in order to have your license reinstated. Acceptable proof includes a DUII Treatment Completion Certificate or a court order indicating that you have completed the required treatment.

CRIME AND CRIMINAL RECORDS

If you are convicted of three DUIIs in five years, your driver's license can be revoked. If you drive after that, you can be convicted of "driving while suspended or revoked."

Like alcohol, marijuana can impair your ability to drive. It's treated the same way as a charge of driving under the influence of intoxicants. As a practical matter, you should know that driving under the influence of marijuana and alcohol together makes you even more dangerous than either substance separately.

G-4. Disturbing the Peace and "Offensive Littering"

Another frequent alcohol-related problem is public urination, especially on Friday and Saturday nights after the bars have closed. You can be cited for offensive littering on public or private property. Throwing trash (like those half-full beer bottles or drug paraphernalia) out of your car also fits the definition of offensive littering. A fine or jail time can result.

G-5. Traffic Offenses

All the rules about driving are designed to anticipate and thus prevent surprises. It's surprises that result in wrecks.

If the police stop you when you're driving, it's most likely because you were speeding, switching lanes without signaling, going through a red light, or doing something like talking on your telephone or texting—all things that lead to dangerous surprises.

If you receive a traffic citation, read the ticket carefully for your options in responding to the ticket. Pay attention to the date that you are scheduled to appear in court. You must either pay the fine (equivalent to pleading guilty) or request a hearing before this court date. If you do not pay and do not appear on your scheduled court date, a default judgment will be entered against you for the full amount written on your ticket, plus additional fees and costs. DMV will also suspend your license. (The judgment will damage your credit; see Section B-1, "Good Credit—Getting It and Keeping It.")

98

If this is your first ticket, immediately call the court at the telephone number listed on your ticket. The court clerk will be able to tell you if you qualify for diversion. Diversion sends you to traffic safety school, and you will not have to pay the fine—unless you miss a session of the traffic safety school. If you do not qualify for diversion, talk to the court clerk about options for reducing your fine. If, at your hearing, the judge concludes that you are not guilty of the offense, the court will return your payment in a few weeks.

If you have a collision with another vehicle, call 911 if anyone is injured. Then exchange your name and address, along with proof of insurance, with the other driver. You should also try to collect the names and addresses of any possible witnesses (including passengers), and take photos or videos of the accident and any damage. If you have car damage or other property damage or medical costs of more than $2,500, you should fill out an accident report within 72 hours with the DMV office.

Under Oregon law, a bicycle is a vehicle. When you ride a bicycle, you must follow the same laws as other "drivers," including laws prohibiting you from operating a vehicle under the influence of intoxicants. When you ride a bicycle, you must follow all speed limit signs and traffic signals. At night, you must have a rear reflector and a white front light. You must signal your upcoming turns. If there's a bike lane, you have to use it. If there's no bike lane, then you must either keep up with traffic or ride as far to the right as possible. Oregon law requires all motor vehicle owners to carry insurance that covers injuries to bicyclists.

G-6. If You Miss Your Court Date

You forgot about court. Your car broke down. You couldn't find a place to park. Your alarm didn't go off. Bottom line: you were late for court to contest a traffic ticket or a more serious offense. Your name is now on a "bench warrant"—an order from a judge to the police that, if they are in contact with you for some other reason, they can arrest you for failing to appear for that underlying case. The charge will be a misdemeanor or a felony, depending on the gravity of the underlying case.

What should you do if you miss your court date? Keep things from getting any worse: immediately call the court clerk's office where your case was scheduled to be heard to ask what to do next. If the clerk says something unhelpful like, "I'm sorry; I can't give you legal advice," then ask to talk to the trial assistant or the secretary of the judge who was scheduled to hear your case, and see if you can work something out.

If you get nowhere, or if the proposed solution is impossible for you to comply with ("Bring $500 in cash to the traffic court cashier by 4:55 p.m. today"), get legal advice immediately. Remember that, if it was a traffic offense, your driver's license is suspended for now.

G-7. Illegal Downloading, File Sharing, and Copyright Violations

Games, movies, TV shows, music, software: downloading media is easy. Seems harmless enough, right? But if what you're downloading is copyrighted, and you're downloading it without permission from the copyright holder, you're engaging in digital piracy.

Federal copyright law prohibits Internet users from getting copies of media that they don't purchase legally. The penalty for illegal downloading can be staggering: up to five years in prison, and fines up to $250,000 per file.

How does anyone know you are illegally downloading copyright-protected media? The Recording Industry Association of America and the Motion Picture Association of America monitor downloads closely, paying particular attention to colleges and universities. If someone uses the campus Internet system to download, these organizations notify the school of the breach. The school then identifies the user and directs the student disciplinary board to take action.

Meanwhile, the Recording Industry Association of America and the Motion Picture Association of America may decide to take legal action. They will contact your Internet service provider to get your name and mailing address, and notify you that they will name you in a lawsuit. Or they will mail you a settlement offer to avoid court, and ask you to contact a settlement hotline or agent. Before responding in any way, immediately get legal advice. The time limit in which to resolve the problem is very short.

If your device has P2P (peer-to-peer) downloading and sharing software, it will default to "share" unless you turn off that feature. If left on, the share feature makes music and movie files available to others to download. You'll be safer if you stay away from illegal sharing software such as Limewire, Kazaa, Bearshare, BitTorrent, and Ares. Legal music downloading is available from Amazon, Yahoo, eMusic, and other sites. Legal movie downloading sites include Amazon, Netflix, Vongo, and Redbox Instant.

Not surprisingly, having shareware on your computer raises the risk of viruses, despite anti-virus software. The risk of identity theft also increases.

If you have wireless service in your dorm room or home, set up security with a strong password. If someone else connects to that router and downloads or shares files illegally, the action will be traced back to you and you'll be liable.

G-8. Clearing Your Record

After any arrest or conviction, including delinquency in juvenile court, the state keeps a permanent record of the offender's history. Some of that information is available to landlords, potential employers for some kinds of jobs, government student financial aid providers, and others. Because having an arrest or conviction record can have a strong negative effect on you in the future, Oregon law has made it possible to clear some arrests and some kinds of offenses from the record and to seal other kinds of records so that they are not public. The process described below applies only to state crimes, not to federal offenses.

Removing arrest and conviction information is known as "expungement," or a "set aside," or "expunction." Once the information is removed from your criminal record, you can treat the arrest, conviction, or juvenile court contact as if it never happened. If you have a conviction set aside, for example, you can state on any job application that you have never been arrested for or convicted of that crime. You also can qualify for certain kinds of student loans and grants if your record is cleared. (It is still possible for some reviewers to find evidence of expunged arrests and convictions in other ways, but expungement still makes a big difference in most cases.)

Courts have discretion whether to permit an expungement. Expunging a juvenile record is easier than expunging an adult criminal record. And getting an arrest set aside is much easier and faster than getting a conviction set aside.

Some criminal records cannot be set aside at all, for example DUII (even after a diversion), traffic offenses, sex crimes, child abuse, most serious felonies, and endangering the welfare of a child. Prosecutors can object to setting aside a conviction. For these reasons, it's important to consult with an attorney about obtaining an expungement, preferably before you have spent money to start the process. A lawyer also can help ensure that all agencies involved in your case set aside the record.

G-9. Crime Victims' Rights

If you are the victim of a crime, you have certain rights with respect to the case against the offender. These rights vary, depending on whether the crime is prosecuted in federal, state, or tribal court. Some rights are automatic; some you get only if you ask for them immediately. In addition, in some cases you may be eligible for compensation from the state for certain expenses related to the crime. The rules regarding your rights are complex; they are not all mentioned here. You will want legal advice about how to proceed.

State law. You have the right to be informed about your rights as a victim of a crime as soon as possible. Often, police will provide you with that information; or you may get it from the victims' assistance staff at the district attorney's office.

You can ask for the right to advance notice of important stages in the case where the defendant will be present in open court. Asking for notice will entitle you to know about and attend release hearings and other pretrial hearings; hearings regarding the defendant's entry of a plea of guilty or no contest; the defendant's trial; and the defendant's sentencing and restitution hearings. You have the right to be heard at pre-trial release and sentencing hearings. If you ask, the prosecutor must consult with you about plea-bargaining in violent felonies. You also have the right to notice of probation and parole hearings, but must request it from the Oregon Board of Parole and Post-Prison Supervision at 503-945-0907.

In some cases, you can ask for testing of the defendant for HIV and other communicable diseases. At your request, your identifying information can be withheld from the defendant unless he or she gets a court order to have it disclosed. You can ask the court to keep the defendant from contacting you. You do not have to speak with the defendant or the defendant's attorney during the case. In some cases, the court must award you restitution from the defendant for your losses.

If you are the victim of a sex offense, you have the right to ask for emergency contraception from a hospital. You may ask the court to keep the media from recording or photographing the legal proceedings.

If you are the victim of a crime involving drunk driving, you can ask for copies of all information related to the case that the defendant receives. You have the right to notice of hearings on the defendant's petition for diversion in lieu of prosecution if the driver damaged your property.

Federal law. If you are the victim of a federal crime, you have the right to advance notice of any public court proceeding or parole hearing involving the crime, and of any release or escape by the defendant. You also have the right to confer with the prosecuting attorney in the case. Normally, you have the right to attend and testify at court hearings, including pre-trial release, plea, and sentencing hearings, and parole proceedings. The court should respect your privacy and seek full restitution for you.

Tribal court. Oregon has nine federally recognized native tribes. Some tribes have their own court systems. The laws of each tribe differ, and it is not possible to generalize in this guide about procedures or victims' rights. Legal advice will be essential.

Compensation for victims. Victims (or others, such as family members who are directly affected) of certain state crimes may get compensation for the harm done to them. They must have reported the crime within 72 hours, and must have cooperated fully with law enforcement in developing the case. There are exceptions to these requirements, for good cause.

Compensation can include medical expenses, counseling, lost earnings, funeral expenses, and loss of support for children and other dependents. Dollar limits apply for each category, and a total dollar limit applies regardless of how many persons qualify for compensation in a particular case. No compensation is available for damage to property.

You must file a formal application for compensation within one year of the crime, unless there is good cause to file later. Your application must include the background of the case and documentation of your expenses. There will be a hearing to determine whether you qualify for compensation, and, if so, for how much money. Having a lawyer can be helpful; free counsel may be available from the Oregon Crime Victims Law Center.

H.

OTHER TOPICS

H-1. "Greek" life—fraternities and sororities

Some colleges and universities host fraternities and sororities. The relationship is often rocky, for several reasons. One reason is that universities want to encourage diversity and inclusion, while these social clubs are by their nature exclusionary. Nationally, more than 75 percent of fraternity and sorority members are white and from upper-income families. (After graduation, these alumni have a built-in business network.) They're more likely to write checks to their alumni association because they remember their fraternity experience fondly. And, on campuses where membership requires that students maintain a minimum GPA, graduation rates among members are higher than they are among the general student population.

"Frat house culture" has a serious downside—with significant legal implications. The level of regular binge drinking is twice that of non-fraternity members. Fraternity members are three times as likely to commit rape. And, every year, thanks primarily to initiation "hazing", fraternity pledges die or are killed by their "brothers." (In 2019, for example, between September and November four fraternity students died from alcohol poisoning or physical injuries related to hazing. Some of their abusers have been charged with homicide.)

Hazing—any combination of physical abuse used to initiate someone into a student organization or to elevate that person to a higher ranking in the organization—

violates state law in Oregon and many other states. It applies not just to fraternities and sororities but also to athletic teams, college bands, etc.

Hazing is so pervasive and so dangerous that 47 national and international "Greek" organizations have established an anti-hazing hotline. Anyone can call to report a suspected hazing incident in a social fraternity, on a team, band, other clubs, etc. The hotline will refer the case immediately to the school for investigation and action. The number is 888-668-4293.

See "Fraternity and sorority housing" for information about residence contracts.

H-2. Small Claims Court

Some kinds of legal problems are solved relatively quickly and cheaply by using small claims court. Oregon small claims court can be used for losses up to $10,000, and, with only a few exceptions, *must* be used for claims under $750. Lawyers generally are not permitted in this "people's court."

Plaintiffs (those who start the lawsuit) and defendants (those getting sued) must pay a filing fee to present their side of the case. If your income is very low, you may be able to file a case or respond to a case by getting a fee waiver or deferral from the court.

Note: You can't use small claims court to ask for your belongings back if your landlord took them. There is a very fast circuit court process for this purpose. Ask the circuit court clerk for help.

When you are the plaintiff. Can you win your case? Before starting your case, do some reading about your rights and, if at all possible, talk to an attorney about whether you are likely to win your case. Without that advice, you may think you have a claim that you don't, or you may not realize how many claims you have.

Remember that in small claims court, you need not only to be in the right, you have to be able to prove that you are in the right. Example: You're suing your former landlord for keeping your apartment security deposit. Do you have photos or witnesses who saw that your apartment was immaculate and undamaged when you moved out? A lawyer can help you figure out what you need to prove your case. See Appendix I, "Getting Help" for tips on research and getting affordable advice.

Also consider whether the amount of your claim is worth the time and effort it will take to prepare your case, and whether you can locate the person or business you want to sue, because you must give that person or business formal notice of your claim.

If you sue someone who then files a claim against you in response to your case, that person may win the case against you. Then you will owe damages and court costs. In certain types of cases, including those involving claims of more than $750, the person you sue may be able to change the case from a small claims case to a circuit court case, where that person could be represented by a lawyer. If you lose the case, you could be liable for that lawyer's fees.

When you are the defendant. If you are being sued in a small claims case, you will get a formal notice of the case either by certified mail or by hand delivery. You have to make some of the same decisions that the plaintiff in your case had to make—only a lot faster. In Oregon, you have only 14 days from the time you receive your court papers in which to fight the case with a formal answer or file your own claim against the plaintiff. If you don't respond to the notice, the plaintiff wins the case automatically, without a hearing. Just like potential plaintiffs, defendants are wise to get some legal advice if they possibly can before deciding whether to fight the claim in court.

Preparing for court. Gather all the information you will need to explain and support your side of the case: names, dates, times, and what people said and did. Put the information in chronological order so you can explain your situation clearly. If you have documents, be sure to have one copy for the court, one for the other side, and one for yourself. If you have witnesses, make sure they know what questions you will ask them. If at all possible, watch other small claims cases before your court date. Read the guidance in the "Getting Help" section of this book for more information.

Mediation. Many Oregon courts offer mediation in small claims court. A trained mediator helps the parties attempt to come to an agreement themselves, without the need for a hearing. People who mediate their cases report that they get better results when they settle outside of court like this.

The hearing. Get to the courthouse at least 30 minutes early so you can park, pass through courthouse security, and find your courtroom. When your case is called, the plaintiff will testify first, call witnesses, and present any documents related to the case. The defendant then presents the other side of the case. The judge may question either the plaintiff or the defendant. The judge will usually make a decision at the end of your hearing. Sometimes a judge will make a decision later, but you can expect to know the outcome very soon. If you win your case, the court does not collect your money for you. You must do that yourself. The collection process can be difficult and expensive.

What if you lose your case? There's no right of appeal from a small claims court decision—except when your small claims case starts out in county justice court rather than in the small claims department of a circuit court. Even there, you can appeal only to the circuit court for a new trial, and only in limited circumstances.

Having a court judgment against you. Most court judgments accrue interest, at the rate of 9 per cent or more. The amount you owe grows quickly, so pay off the judgment as fast as you can. In addition, court judgments go into your credit report and stay there for years, affecting your ability to borrow money, get work, housing, insurance, and some kinds of employment. For more information, see Section B-1, "Good Credit—Getting It and Keeping It."

H-3. Authorizing Others to Make Decisions

Planning for future problems can prevent future problems. For example, how do you protect your rights and your wishes if you plan to study abroad? If you are called up to active military duty and will be away from home? If you are in a horrific traffic crash that leaves you unable to speak or to write? If you need to leave your children with someone else for a while?

In each of these situations, a power of attorney (POA) that you create now can help you out later. A POA is a legal document that authorizes someone you choose to make certain kinds of decisions for you if you can't be reached. There are several kinds of POAs.

A general power of attorney gives another person the right to conduct all kinds of business and financial matters for you. You can cancel (revoke) the power at any time. While a general power may be appropriate in some cases, it is often best to use a limited power of attorney.

A limited power of attorney authorizes someone else to do certain things for you—for example, deposit checks in your checking account, write checks to cover your monthly bills, etc. You can revoke the power at any time.

A power of attorney described in more detail in Section E-4, "Child Care for Extended Periods," gives someone else the authority to register your child in school and get medical care for the child. It is valid for up to six months (longer, if you are on active military duty) and can be renewed indefinitely. Like other powers, it can be revoked at any time.

Health care powers of attorney. Oregon law provides for health care decision-making in an official form for this purpose, available at Oregon hospitals and medical offices. The form has two parts—an advance directive that tells medical providers what your wishes are; and the naming of a health care representative, whose duty is to see that medical providers carry out your wishes if you can't tell the providers yourself. You can revoke this power, too, or change representatives.

H-4. LGBTQ Issues

Discrimination. The Oregon Equality Act forbids discrimination based on sexual orientation, gender identity, or gender expression (including where it differs from behavior traditionally associated with your assigned sex at birth) in these realms:

1. Employment—all public and private employers;
2. Housing—renting, purchasing, or improving real estate;
3. Public accommodations—all places open to the public, such as stores, restaurants, arenas, parks, campgrounds, hotels, hospitals, doctor offices, etc.;

4.   Financial matters—insurance and credit applications;

5.   Public education;

6.   Foster parenting and adoption;

7.   Jury duty;

8.   Correctional facilities and programs;

9.   Custody and parenting time; and

10. Medical treatment.

If you are the victim of violence based on perceptions about your sexual orientation, gender identity, or gender expression, that violence can be prosecuted as a hate crime, with enhanced penalties.

Relationship violence. Violent relationships aren't limited to heterosexual couples. Help is available through local domestic violence/rape intervention programs and non-hetero abuse survivor networks. See Appendix I, "Getting Help."

Name change. If you're forging a new gender identity, you may want a name that fits that identity. Anyone in Oregon can get a name change easily, so long as the change isn't "contrary to the public interest." What's that mean? Courts have said, for example, that they would not permit registered sex offenders to change their names to make it harder for potential victims to know they were sex offenders.

You can file an application for a name change with your local probate court. There's a filing fee, which varies from county to county. After the court grants the order for the new name, you submit a certified copy of the order showing your new name to the Oregon Vital Records office. You can deliver or mail it to:

Vital Records and Certificates
Oregon Center for Health Statistics
Oregon Health Agency
P.O. Box 14050
800 NE Oregon St
Portland OR 97232

There's a fee ($35 in 2020) to get the Vital Records file amended. Don't forget to update your driver's license with DMV, your voter registration (on a separate form but also through DMV), and your Social Security records with the Social Security office (see its website for instructions). You may need additional certified copies of your name change order for these purposes.

Sex change. The probate court has the power to change the record of your legally recognized sex at your request. To apply to the court for a change of legal sex, you must show that you have undergone surgical, hormonal, or other treatment appropriate for the purpose of your gender transition, and that your sexual reassignment has been completed. ("Other treatment" can be as simple as counseling for transsexual gender reassignment, without medical intervention, lawyers have reported.) You must submit a document from a physician or a qualified therapist.

You can seek a change of assigned sex at the same time you ask the probate court for a name change. Again, be sure to notify DMV, and update your voter registration. At some point, you also will need to update your Social Security information—see its website for instructions.

If you plan to travel abroad, you'll have to update your passport or obtain one showing your new identity. Apply through the passport agency of the U.S. Department of State; include a very specific statement signed by your physician. Expect roadblocks, and allow several months for this process to be completed.

The law isn't clear yet about the legal effects of transitioning while married or in a registered domestic partnership, and whether transgendered individuals can use bathrooms, locker rooms, memberships, and pricing discounts consistent with gender expression in places of public accommodation.

H-5. "Dreamers" and DACA

The Deferred Action for Childhood Arrivals Act, passed during the Obama Administration, has protected immigrant children of undocumented immigrants from deportation, making it possible for them to get higher education and enter the job market. The Trump Administration intends to end the program. The

United States Supreme Court decided in June 2020 that the government did not give proper justification to end it, but there may be another challenge before the year is over.

H-6. Legal Issues for International Students

Dealing with the police. Section G-1, "Dealing with the Police," applies to all students. As someone from another country, you may be surprised by some of the things that the police expect here. For example, if the police stop the car you are in, they expect you to stay in the car. Do not open the car door; do not get out unless the police ask you to. Everyone in the car should keep their hands visible. Do not move suddenly.

If the police talk as if they are going to give a ticket (or citation) to the driver of the car, no one in the car should offer to pay the fine to the police. No one should ever offer to give the police money. In the United States, it is a crime to try to "bribe" the police. The police will assume that is what you are doing if you offer money. All fines must be paid to the court. (The ticket will describe how to pay.)

If you receive a ticket, it is especially important for you not to miss your court date and time. Not showing up can mean that your visa will be revoked and that, if you leave the United States, you may not be able to get back in.

Your visa also may be revoked if you are convicted of a crime in the United States.

Your identification papers. As an international student, you will have either an F-1 or a J-1 visa. You may see that your American friends do not need to carry their citizenship papers with them. As a visitor, however, you must always carry your papers with you. Pay attention to the expiration date of your passport; if it expires less than six months before the end of your program, be sure to get it renewed. If you have a driver's license or other documents that show your Oregon address, be sure to update that address right away if you move.

Your student visa is valid while you are a full-time student. Once you graduate, you may stay in the United States for up to 60 days (starting on the last day of your final term) if you have an F-1 visa, or up to 30 days if you have a J-1 visa. If you stay past that date, your visa will no longer be valid; you may not be able to get your status back.

Working part-time while in school. International students can participate in paid or unpaid internships. They also can work for pay, up to 20 hours per week with on-campus employers (book store, dining hall, university offices, etc.) during the regular school year and 40 hours per week during summer break. If you find a part-time job, you must notify the international program on your campus BEFORE you start working. See Section C, "Your Rights in the Workplace," to learn about your rights as intern or employee.

Communicating with the international program on campus. Staff at the international program office can help you keep your student visa while you work toward graduation, but that staff relies on you to keep their records current. Contact the program in advance if you:

— Want to change your degree program or major;
— Want to participate in post-graduation practical training;
— Are going to move to a new address;
— Want to get a job while a student;
— Want to transfer to a different university;
— Need help to extend or renew your passport; or
— Are contacted by a United States immigration official.

Getting legal advice about your immigration status. Staff at the international program office at your college or university can answer many questions, but only a lawyer trained in immigration law can give you accurate information about your status. You may have questions not only about your student status, but also about marriage, having children, criminal law, and other topics that are complicated if you are not a citizen or a permanent legal resident of the United States. See Appendix I, "Getting Help", for more information.

H-7. Voting

You can register to vote in Oregon if you're a U.S. citizen and live in the state. What does it mean to "live in the state"? It's the place you consider home while you are in school. As a student, you might live in your parents' home or somewhere else off-campus, or in a dorm on campus. You must register at least 21 days before the first election in which you want to vote. (Being a resident for voting is not the same as being a resident for in-state tuition.)

If you live on campus and provide a campus address as your residential (physical) address on your voter registration form, be sure to use your dormitory and room number; a P.O. Box is not a residential address. Oregonians vote by mail, so your ballot will go to your mailing address. Your ballot can be sent to you anywhere in the world, even if you are participating in a study-abroad program.

Note that, when you change your name or your address, you must update your DMV records. That agency has online forms for both purposes.

If you are registered to vote in another state but qualify to vote in Oregon, be sure to cancel your registration in that other state when you register to vote in Oregon. And don't be tempted to vote in both states—it's a felony. The Oregon Secretary of State has more information. See https://sos.oregon.gov/voting/Pages/voteinor.aspx

H-8. Student Discipline

Every college has some kind of student discipline office to deal with violations of school rules—rules against cheating (which includes helping others cheat), theft, abusive conduct, alcohol and drug misuse, etc. The rules may be part of a university-wide code of conduct, or they may be a contractual duty that you take on by living in a dorm, or they may be rules specific to a particular course or even to a particular instructor. The school has the right to sanction students—allowing a grade to be changed to an F, for example, or to require a student whose behavior is disruptive or dangerous to take only online classes, or to suspend or expel a student for severe misconduct.

To be enforceable, all school rules must be in writing and be clear enough to be understood by a reasonable person. Failure to read a rule that's been provided doesn't excuse misconduct.

Before taking action, the disciplinary board or official will give the student an opportunity to explain what happened. At some schools, the student may be able to appeal an unfavorable decision to the dean of students or other designated official. In rare cases, students have filed lawsuits to challenge a school's decision.

If you are subject to discipline and ask for a meeting with the discipline official, be courteous. Be forthright about what happened; don't leave out important details. Most important: Don't lie. The cover-up is itself misconduct, and it's often worse than the misconduct it's designed to hide.

A note about the fallout from academic misconduct: Teachers want to be supportive of students and feel proud of student progress. They are often the first adults students can turn to for references for employment or graduate school. Once you've betrayed their trust in you, they're not likely to recommend you until they see changed behavior.

H-9. "I got court papers!"

You may get official legal documents for a variety of reasons. Your spouse wants a divorce. Your old landlord is taking you to small claims court. You have jury duty. You were a witness to a crime and got subpoenaed.

Read the documents. If they name you as a defendant or a respondent in a court case, they will say how much time you have to file an answer or other response. See a lawyer to discuss your options—and don't wait to do so! If you've been called for Oregon jury duty in the middle of mid-term exams, you can ask for one extension so you can serve later. If you witnessed a car wreck or a robbery, etc., you will have to appear at a trial or a hearing.

Do not ignore any court papers you receive. You can be held in contempt of court for doing so—and face stiff fines.

I.

GETTING HELP

Resources are listed below by topic, followed by a section on finding legal help.

A. Housing Discrimination

Fair Housing Council of Oregon
www.fhco.org
503-223-8197

Oregon Bureau of Labor and Industries
https://www.oregon.gov/boli/CRD/pages/index.aspx
971-673-0761

Oregon State Bar Information for the Public—Housing Discrimination
https://www.osbar.org/public/legalinfo/1248_HousingDiscrimination.htm

OregonLawHelp
https://oregonlawhelp.org/issues/housing/housing-discrimination

B. Landlord-Tenant Law

Oregon State Bar Information for the Public—Landlord-Tenant Law
https://www.osbar.org/public/legalinfo.html#landlordtenant

OregonLawHelp
https://oregonlawhelp.org/issues/housing

Community Alliance of Tenants
Renters' Rights Hotline (Multnomah, Coos,
Jackson, Washington counties)
https://oregoncat.org
503-288-0130

C. Fraternity/Campus Organization Hazing

National Anti-Hazing Hotline (24-hour)
888-668-4293

Emergency Help
911

D. Utilities

Oregon Public Utilities Commission
www.oregon.gov/PUC
800-692-7380

E. Consumer Rights

Oregon Attorney General Consumer Protection
https://www.doj.state.or.us/consumer-protection/
877-877-9392

National Consumer Law Center
www.nclc.org

OregonLawHelp
https://oregonlawhelp.org/issues/consumer/consumer-protection-and-complaints

Oregon State Bar Information for the Public—Consumer Law
https://www.osbar.org/public/legalinfo.html#consumerrights

F. Debts and Debt Collection

OregonLawHelp
https://oregonlawhelp.org/issues/consumer/debt-collection-garnishment-repos-session

Oregon State Bar Information for the Public—Debtors' Rights
https://www.osbar.org/public/legalinfo/1021_DebtorsRights.htm

G. Bankruptcy

Oregon State Bar Information for the Public
https://www.osbar.org/public/legalinfo/bankruptcy.html

OregonLawHelp
https://oregonlawhelp.org/issues/consumer/bankruptcy

U.S. Bankruptcy Court for the District of Oregon
https://www.orb.uscourts.gov/

H. Student Loans

National Consumer Law Center Student Loan Assistance Program
https://www.studentloanborrowerassistance.org/

The College Board
www.collegeboard.org

I. Employment Rights

Oregon Bureau of Labor and Industries
https://www.oregon.gov/boli/CRD/pages/index.aspx
971-673-0761

OregonLawHelp
https://oregonlawhelp.org/issues/work

Oregon State Bar Information for the Public—LGBTQ rights
https://www.osbar.org/public/legalinfo.html#lgbtq

Oregon State Bar Information for the Public—Disability Rights
https://www.osbar.org/public/legalinfo/1095_DiscriminationEmployOpps.htm

J. Pregnancy and Contraception

Planned Parenthood
https://www.plannedparenthood.org/health-center/or

Campus Health Centers

K. Domestic and Sexual Assault Victims Services

Oregon Coalition for Domestic and Sexual Violence
https://ocadsv.org/find-help

Northwest Network of Bi, Trans, Lesbian, and Gay Survivors of Abuse
https://www.nwnetwork.org

National Domestic Violence Hotline
800-799-SAFE

National Sexual Assault Hotline
800-656-HOPE

Oregon State Bar Information for the Public—Domestic Violence Restraining Orders
https://www.osbar.org/public/legalinfo/1140_RestrainingOrders.htm

OregonLawHelp
https://oregonlawhelp.org/issues/protection-from-abuse

Oregon Circuit Court restraining order forms and information
https://www.courts.oregon.gov/courts/Pages/default.aspx

Women's Resource Centers on campus; LGBTQ on-campus programs

L. Family law

Oregon Circuit Court family law forms and information
https://www.courts.oregon.gov/courts/Pages/default.aspx

OregonLawHelp
https://oregonlawhelp.org/issues/family

Oregon State Bar Information for the Public—Family Law
https://www.osbar.org/public/legalinfo.html#family

M. Crime and Criminal Records

Oregon State Bar Information for the Public—Expunging Criminal and Juvenile
Records
https://www.osbar.org/public/legalinfo/1081_ClearingRecord.htm

OregonLawHelp
https://oregonlawhelp.org/resource/what-does-expunging-my-criminal-record-
in-oregon-mean-and-what-do-i-do-next

ACLU: Stopped by Police?
https://www.aclu.org/know-your-rights/stopped-by-police/

Oregon State Bar Information for the Public—Criminal Law
https://www.osbar.org/public/legalinfo.html#criminal

N. Crime Victims' Rights

Oregon Department of Justice
https://www.doj.state.or.us/crime-victims/victims-rights/victims-rights-guides/

O. Court Information

Circuit Courts in Oregon
https://courts.oregon.gov/courts/Pages/default.aspx

Using Small Claims Court in Oregon 2d Ed (Oregon Legal Guides)

Oregon State Bar Program, "All Rise! Taking Your Case to Small Claims Court" video
https://www.osbar.org/public/legalinfo/1061_SmallClaims.htm

P. Mediation Programs

Oregon Mediation Association
ormediation.org

Q. Voting Rights

Oregon Secretary of State
https://sos.oregon.gov/voting/pages/voteinor.aspx

GETTING LEGAL ADVICE

On-Campus Legal Services for Students: University of Oregon, Oregon State University, Portland State University, Southern Oregon University, Lane Community College

Law School Legal Clinic Programs: Willamette University, University of Oregon

Legal Aid Programs for Low-Income Persons, see
www.oregonlawhelp.org for locations statewide

Oregon State Bar Lawyer Referral Service
800-452-7636
Reduced-fee initial consultation in many topic areas

ACLU of Oregon
www.aclu-or.org
Services limited to First Amendment, police misconduct, and other Bill-of-Rights
issues

II.

DEFINITIONS OF LEGAL TERMS

Advance directive for health care—document that directs medical providers to provide or withhold certain treatments when a person is unable to make decisions.

Answer—in a lawsuit, this is a document a defendant who fights the claims must file with the court within a certain period of time.

Arrest—to take a person into custody in a criminal case and charge the person with a crime.

Bankruptcy—court proceeding to reduce or eliminate debt that debtor cannot pay

Bench warrant—an arrest warrant a judge can issue when a person fails to appear at a hearing in a criminal case.

Circuit court—in Oregon, the general court in each county.

Civil case—a lawsuit filed by one person or entity against another person or entity

Common area—in rental housing, areas like lawns and stairways and elevators and parking lots that are open to all residents.

Common-law marriage—legal marriage without a ceremony, recognized by only a few states.

Consensual sex—sexual contact between willing adults.

Consolidation—of loans, combining two or more loans to reduce monthly payments over a longer period of time, generally at a higher interest rate.

Consumer Price Index (CPI)—an economic measurement of increases and decreases in some consumer costs.

Contest—in a civil case, to file an answer or other document to show that defendant disagrees with what plaintiff is seeking and wants a trial or hearing.

Contraband—illegal items. It can include weapons, drugs, explosives, chemicals, and, for minors, alcohol.

Contract—agreement that can be enforced by a court order.

Co-sign—take on responsibility to pay back a loan or take on other responsibility because the person who wants it cannot get approved by the creditor.

Credit bureau—credit reporting agency.

Credit history—records of a person's payment history for most kinds of loans or other periodic payments.

Credit reporting agency—business that tracks debts and payments to establish an individual's creditworthiness, that is, whether a person should be allowed to borrow money.

Credit report—record of payments of debts by individuals maintained by credit reporting agencies.

Creditor—someone who is owed money.

Criminal case—case that government brings against an individual or entity after likely violation of criminal law in that jurisdiction.

Cure—fix a problem or make a problem stop.

Custody, of children—status of having primary physical responsibility for minor children by one parent.

Damages—in a civil case, an amount of money that a court orders someone to pay. Damages include special damages such as an amount ordered by law (also called statutory damages), compensatory (to make up for profits or wages, etc., lost as a result of the conduct giving rise to the case),punitive damages (payment in excess of other damages, ordered to discourage continued severe misconduct), and general damages (pain and suffering, indignity).

Default—in a civil case, when defendant/respondent does not file an answer, plaintiff gets what he or she asked for without a trial or hearing.

Defendant—person who is sued. Also, the accused in a criminal case.

Discrimination—different treatment based on reasons that are against the law.

Dismiss—court throws out a case because the plaintiff had no right to file it; can apply in both civil and criminal cases.

Diversion—in a traffic case or Driving under the Influence (DUI) case, some first offenses can qualify for treatment or safety training.

Eviction—court order requiring tenant to move out of rented property.

Exempt property—property belonging to a judgment debtor that a creditor has no right to garnish.

Expungement, expunction—removal of offenses from a criminal record.

Family Abuse Protection Act Order—court order prohibiting future contact with a victim of domestic violence.

Felony—serious crime that can result in at least a year of prison, as well as fines and other penalties.

Filing fee—in all civil (non-criminal) cases, courts charge a fee to file petitions or complaints and answers to those claims.

Filing fee waiver, deferral—persons whose incomes and assets are very small can file or respond in a civil case after getting a judge to sign a waiver or deferral form.

Finance—to finance a purchase is to borrow money to pay for it, usually in installments.

First appearance—in FED case, tenant's appearance in court to ask for a trial. In criminal case, a first appearance is usually known as an arraignment, where a defendant learns what the charges are and can ask for an attorney.

Forcible entry and detainer (FED)—court case to determine if landlord has right to evict tenant.

Garnishment—judgment creditor's right to take a portion of a debtor's income from work or money from accounts in order to get repayment of a debt.

Gate fee—small charge a towing company can require of a vehicle owner to enter the storage lot when the lot is closed.

Habitable—referring to a rental unit, meaning fit to live in (as defined by ORLTA)

Harassment—criminal conduct toward another person that is severely annoying, or causes the person to be fearful.

Hate crime—criminal act that includes an element of choosing victim based on discriminatory intent.

Impound—take possession of someone's property for safekeeping.

Inventory—complete list of items in an impounded vehicle or other property

Joint legal custody—sharing of decision-making for children by both parents.

Judgment creditor—someone who is owed money and has obtained a court judgment to enforce the right to collect the debt.

Judgment debtor—someone who a court says owes money to another.

Judgment—final order (decision) of a court in a civil case.

Last month's rent—a rent payment a landlord requires in advance of accepting a tenant in addition to first month's rent and that the landlord can apply to the final month of the tenancy.

Lease—rental agreement. Lease usually means an agreement that ends on a particular date (a term lease), but can include month-to-month rental agreements.

Liable, liability—in a non-criminal case, fault or responsibility. It also indicates responsibility to pay for damage or harm done to another.

Mechanic's lien—right of a car mechanic to retain and sell a vehicle if the owner does not pay for repairs.

Misdemeanor—crime that can result in up to a year of prison, along with fines and other penalties.

Monetary penalty—type of damages set out by statute; for example, a landlord who unlawfully keeps a former tenant's security deposit is liable for a penalty of twice the amount withheld.

Non-competition agreement—agreement an employer requires an employee to sign before starting a new job, prohibiting the employee from working for a similar employer for a certain period of time or certain territory or both.

Non-disclosure agreement—agreement an employer requires an employee to sign before starting a new job, prohibiting the employee from making certain kinds of information available to persons other than the employer.

Notice—prescribed way to give someone information, for example, notice of a rent increase, notice of habitability problems, etc. Depending on the situation, a notice can be oral or written. It can sometimes be required before a person takes someone else to court.

Oregon Residential Landlord and Tenant Act (ORLTA)—state law that applies to residential tenancies.

Parenting time—time periods when parent has court-ordered right to spend time with parent's children.

Plaintiff—person who files a case in court against someone else in a civil case.

Power of attorney—document that allows a person to authorize someone else to make decisions. A general power of attorney gives the person sweeping powers; a limited power of attorney authorizes only certain actions.

Protected status, protected class—a category of individuals who are protected by law against unlawful discrimination.

Public assistance—need-based help from the government, such as food stamps, Medicaid, subsidized rent, etc.

Public utilities—electricity, water, gas companies or cooperatives.

Recall—manufacturers or dealers who know about a serious defect in a product take it back and repair or replace it.

Registered sex offender—a person convicted of certain sex crimes who must register his or her whereabouts as part of a public record, and is restricted from living in certain locations and working in certain positions.

Rent control—a limit a government imposes on amounts or amount of increases in rent.

Renter's insurance—insurance obtained by tenants to cover loss of their own property and damage they cause to the rental unit.

Repossess—take back an item from a buyer if the buyer does not make agreed-on payments and seller and buyer have a security agreement.

Sanction—penalty, including damages and injunction (an order to stop illegal conduct), a court can impose against a wrong-doer. Also, criminal law punishment.

Satisfaction of money award—also called a satisfaction of judgment, filed with the court, shows that creditor has received some or all of the payment due under the judgment against the debtor.

Security agreement—a signed document that allows a seller to repossess an item if the buyer does not make all the payments on time.

Security deposit—payment a landlord can require in addition to rent payments, money that belongs to the tenant unless the landlord must use it at the end of the tenancy to make repairs of damage caused by the tenant, or to cover unpaid rent.

Sexual Abuse Protective Order—court order prohibiting future contact with a victim of sex abuse.

Sexual assault—any unwanted sexual contact, including some that is criminal, some that is only a civil wrong (**tort**).

Sexual harassment (at work)—includes being forced to engage in sexual activity with a superior or risk loss of job, promotion, or other benefit, and a hostile work environment, where an employee is subject to words and actions based on sex by superiors, co-workers, even customers, visitors, etc.

Sole custody—having primary physical responsibility and decision-making responsibility for minor children by one parent.

Stalking—crime of repeated unwanted following, contact, etc. that would put a reasonable person in fear.

Statute of limitations—a time period the law allows for someone to file a case or for the government to charge a person with a crime.

Stop—right of police to detain a person when police reasonably suspect the person of a crime or other violation of law, e.g., a traffic stop.

Subpoena—order to appear in court (as witness, juror, etc.).

Suspension, of driver license—temporary loss of driving privileges.

Warrant—permission from a court for police to arrest (arrest warrant) or search a person, place, or property (search warrant) based on probable cause a crime has been committed.

Writ of garnishment—formal notice to a judgment debtor that a judgment creditor is attempting to garnish wages or accounts.

INDEX

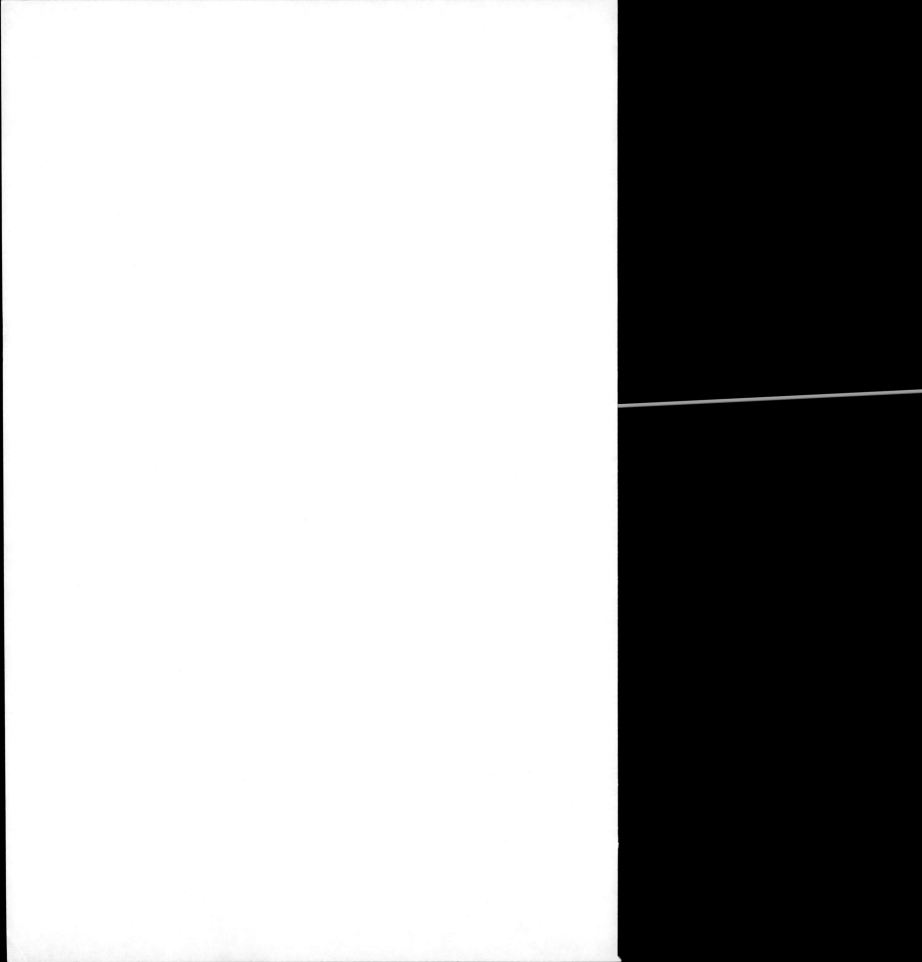

Made in United States
Troutdale, OR
11/09/2023

14438016R00077